1980S**ROCK**RHYTHM GUITAR**MASTERY**

The Ultimate Guide to Powerful Rhythm Guitar & Genre-Defining Riffs

CHRIS**BROOKS**

FUNDAMENTAL**CHANGES**

1980s Rock Rhythm Guitar Mastery

The Ultimate Guide to Powerful Rhythm Guitar & Genre-Defining Riffs

Published by **www.fundamental-changes.com**

ISBN: 978-1-78933-419-7

Copyright © 2023 Christopher A. Brooks

Edited by Tim Pettingale

www.fundamental-changes.com

Facebook: **ChrisBrooksGuitar**

Instagram: **chrisbrooksguitarist**

Join our free Facebook Community of Cool Musicians

www.facebook.com/groups/fundamentalguitar

Tag us for a share on Instagram: **FundamentalChanges**

Cover Image Copyright: Shutterstock, Netfalls Remy

Contents

Introduction 4

Get the Audio 5

Chapter One: What's in the Box 6

Chapter Two: The Big Chorus 16

    Creating Rock Chord Progressions 19

    Modulating Progressions 24

    Tips for creating chord progressions for your songs 29

Chapter Three: Fun Size Chord Fragments 30

    Major Chord Fragmentation 30

    Minor Chord Fragmentation 39

Chapter Four: Hone Your Rhythm Chops 46

Chapter Five: Sparkly Clean Chord Parts 57

    Creative Clean Parts 57

    Tips for writing creative, clean rhythm parts 67

Chapter Six: Scalar Riffs and Harmonies 68

    Suggestions for creating your own scalar riffs 79

Conclusion 88

About the Author 89

Other titles by Chris Brooks 89

Introduction

Rip some holes in your skinny jeans and get out your headbands – it's time to riff out like it's 1987!

Welcome to *1980s Rock Rhythm Guitar Mastery*, a deep dive into creating authentic 1980s hard rock and metal rhythm parts, from the glammed-up Sunset Strip to the fist-raising Bay Area thrash sounds.

The '80s was the decade of BIG: big sounds, big hair, and big riffs! The decade of excess saw chops get faster, guitar rigs get bigger with the boom of rack gear and modified valve amps, and rock music dominate the radio airwaves and MTV.

'80s rock gave us multiple subgenres, including arena rock like Bon Jovi and Def Leppard, glam metal like Poison and Mötley Crüe, post-Van Halen rock like Winger and Ratt, the sleaze of Guns N' Roses and Faster Pussycat, the Euro-metal sounds of Judas Priest and Iron Maiden, and the thrash revolution led by Metallica, Slayer and Megadeth.

Each subgenre of '80s rock had its own influences, subculture and, in many cases, geographic roots.

While other cool things were happening in the '80s, like U2, The Police, The Cure, The Pretenders and more, I'll focus here on the rock and harder-edged side.

This book aims not to spoon-feed you a bunch of soundalike riffs but to help you think like the players who created this kind of rock, from their influences to harmonic choices, their technical approaches, and compositional devices.

Each chapter tackles a different element of '80s rock rhythm playing and riff creation, from pentatonic frameworks to fragmented chord usage, picking hands chops and control, to creating lush, clean parts. So, not only will you better understand the ideas behind your favourite riffs, you'll be able to create your own.

Since there's a somewhat chronological order to many of the concepts presented, I suggest studying the chapters ahead in order. You won't lose too much by bouncing around for fun, but I have structured an order that best serves the developing rhythm player.

To master each riff, work on it unaccompanied and without a metronome until you are playing the notes accurately and with a steady rhythm. Then, try playing to a metronome or a drumbeat, beginning at a comfortable pace and aiming for the performance speeds in the included audio files.

I play each example to the accompaniment in the audio files, calling out the tempo before each track begins. After a couple of repeats, you'll hear my guitars drop out, so you can take over and play along. Faster, more intricate parts will be demonstrated at two speeds, and you can also use free programs like Audacity to change the tempo to your liking.

To start playing sooner, Chapter One begins with minimal preamble.

Jump in, rock out! I hope you enjoy working through each stage of the book.

Chris Brooks

Get the Audio

The audio files for this book are available to download for free from **www.fundamental-changes.com.** The link is in the top right-hand corner. Simply select this book title from the drop-down menu and follow the instructions to get the audio.

We recommend that you download the files directly to your computer, not to your tablet, and extract them there before adding them to your media library. You can then put them on your tablet, iPod or burn them to CD. On the download page, there is a help PDF, and we also provide technical support via the contact form.

For over 350 free guitar lessons with videos check out:

www.fundamental-changes.com

Join our free Facebook Community of Cool Musicians

www.facebook.com/groups/fundamentalguitar

Tag us for a share on Instagram: **FundamentalChanges**

Chapter One: What's in the Box

Taking influence from the rock of the 1960s and '70s, many guitarists of the '80s relied heavily on the pentatonic scale as a staple for riffs and solos, adding tonal and rhythmic elements that contributed to what we now know as the '80s sound.

In this chapter, I'll show you how to use the humble minor pentatonic and minor blues scales as vehicles for creating authentic sounding '80s riffs.

First, let's look for some chords that lurk within the first minor pentatonic box. Here's the G Minor Pentatonic scale, followed by the minor blues variant (which we'll revisit later).

Figure 1: G Minor Pentatonic and G Minor Blues scales

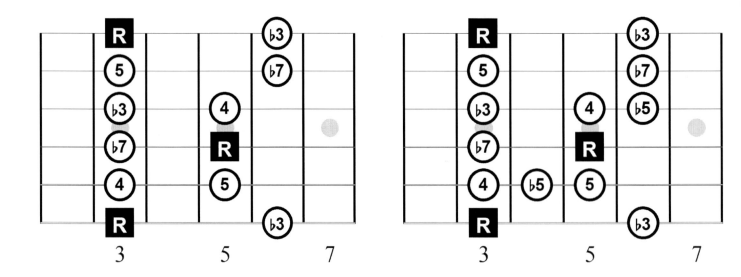

As music in the late '60s and '70s got louder with the emergence of high-wattage amplification and bigger drum kits, it became commonplace for rock bands to write songs around 1/8th note basslines, driving drumbeats and guitar riffs that either pumped along with the bass or overlayed power chords atop the rhythm section. Deep Purple's *Highway Star* and *Smoke on the Water* are classic examples.

Instead of moving regular power chord shapes around the fretboard, guitarists like Ritchie Blackmore often called upon "inverted power chords" within the pentatonic scale.

Where the familiar power chord is played using the root and 5th (with optional octave root on top), inverted power chords are played using the 5th on the bottom. See Example 1a to compare.

Inverted power chord shapes look like perfect 4th intervals, but because the higher note is still the root, we continue to treat them as power chords and name them as such.

I'll indicate inverted power chords with slash symbols like G5/D in the first couple of examples. Afterwards, as we progress and chords become more like moving parts in a busy arrangement, simplified chord symbols will apply.

Looking at the G minor pentatonic box above, we can quickly locate the inverted power chords of F5, G5, Bb5, and C5, playing each with only one finger at a time.

Example 1a:

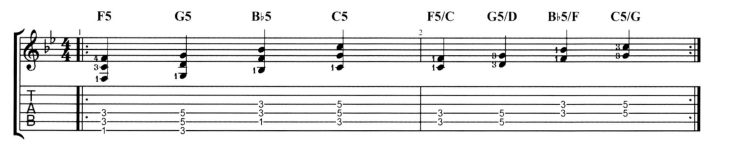

Adding some rhythm and mixing up the order of the chords gets us into Deep Purple and early Whitesnake territory.

Played over a pumping G note on bass and an Ian Paice-style drum part on the audio track, Example 1b sounds like real music already. We're not in the '80s yet, but we will be soon enough!

Example 1b:

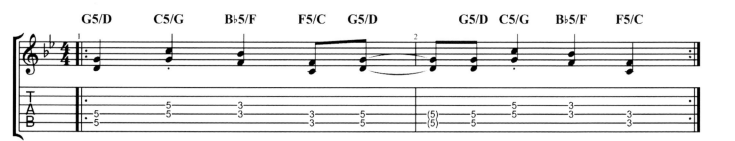

Despite disco and punk both having their runs in the 1970s, the rise of AC/DC's hard blues-rock in the second half of the decade and the emergence of the mighty Van Halen in 1978 proved that hard rock guitar was still just getting started.

In the UK, bands like Judas Priest gained momentum through the late '70s as they ascended to international success through the '80s. Many consider "Priest" an essential link between the first wave of British rock bands and the fully-fledged heavy metal genre.

Stateside, the riffs got faster as the hair got bigger and jeans got tighter (or were replaced with leather!). California's Sunset Strip became the mecca of bands drawing influence from the meat-and-potatoes rock of AC/DC, the flash of Van Halen, and the bold image of '70s glam rock.

Demonstrating an '80s approach to inverted power chords, here's a Mötley Crüe-style riff with some syncopation (anticipating the beginning of each bar), percussive pick strokes, and slides.

Example 1c:

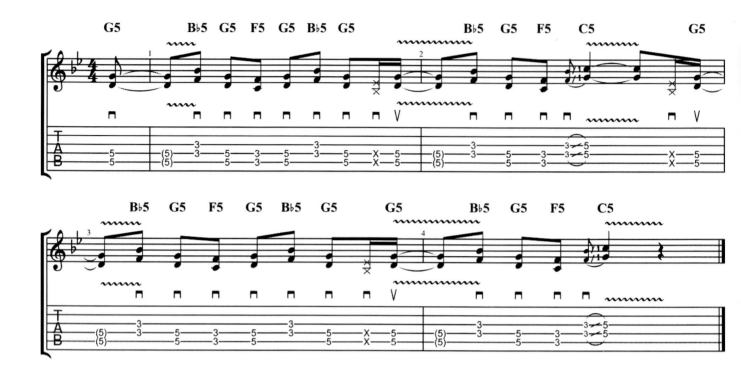

To take your riffing to the next level, palm muting is a great tool to have at your disposal.

If you haven't muted before, place the side of your picking hand on the edge of the strings at the bridge, enough to dampen the sound of the string, while still having the pitch of the fretted note. It will look something like Figure 1b.

Figure 1b:

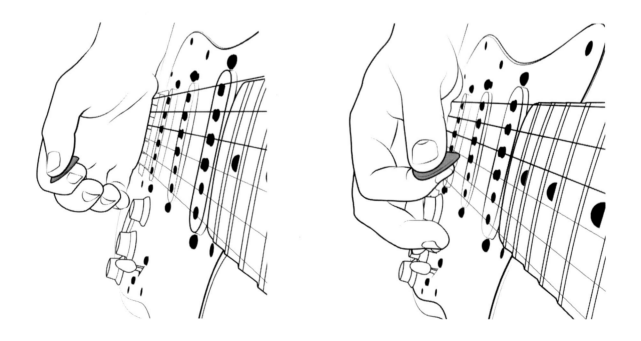

With the palm mute in place, work Example 1d up to a minimum of 150 beats per minute (bpm). If you can do it faster, even better!

Example 1d:

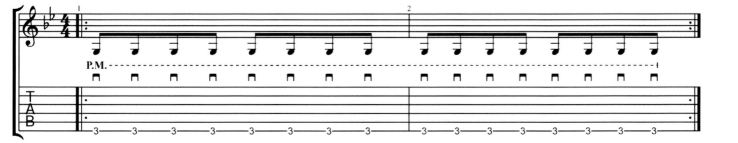

An important next step is deactivating the mute to punctuate with some chord stabs. In this example, the mute is released each time the A and D strings of the G5 power chord are struck.

Example 1e:

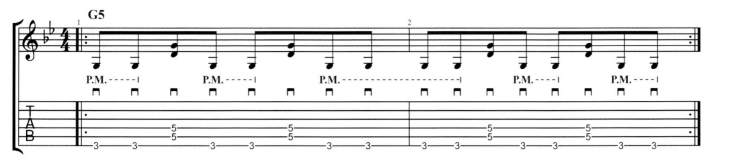

Now that your muting is coming along, we can beef up riffs like Example 1b with some intermittent root note chugging. This common device allows us to lock in with the bass while adding the chordal movement of the inverted power chords.

Here's that earlier riff, reworked. It's now more Judas Priest than Deep Purple.

While the whole riff can be fretted with the first and third fingers, I incorporate the remaining fingers to avoid too much first finger barring. We'll embellish this riff even further shortly.

Example 1f:

Open strings make pedalled bass notes even more straightforward, so it's common to see riffs taking advantage of the open E and A strings.

Example 1g is in the key of A Minor and uses regular and inverted power chords on the D and G strings. See if you can work this one up to 170bpm using all downstrokes. I'll give you two speeds on the backing track while you work on it.

In bar four, the 5th fret of the A string is played as an artificial or "pinch" harmonic. To create the squeal effect, plant the pick into the D string as it leaves the A string, allowing the skin of your thumb to contact the A string while it's still ringing. Then, move your hand out of the way to let the harmonic sound. The thumb's contact point along the string determines the pitch of the harmonic.

Example 1g:

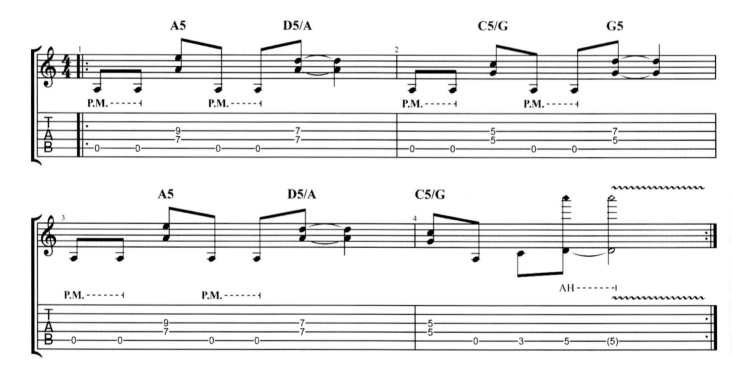

To build your picking hand chops further, add alternate picked 1/16th notes. This drill switches between all downward picked 1/8th notes and alternate picking, muted throughout.

Example 1h:

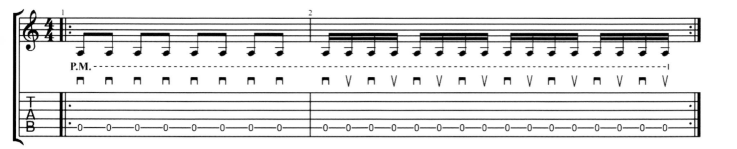

See what tempo you can reach with the next drill which has a different phrase on each beat. In later chapters, we'll get more into this by introducing a range of "galloping" riffs that conjure up the sounds of Iron Maiden, Metallica, and Slayer.

Example 1i:

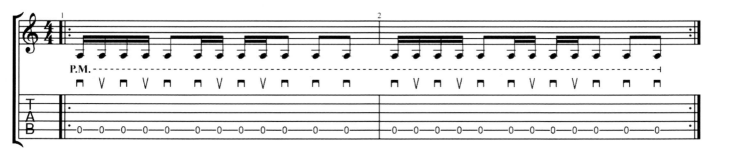

We can create a busier version of Example 1g by adding 1/16th notes. The chords remain in the same spots as before but with twice the number of pedalled A notes.

Example 1j:

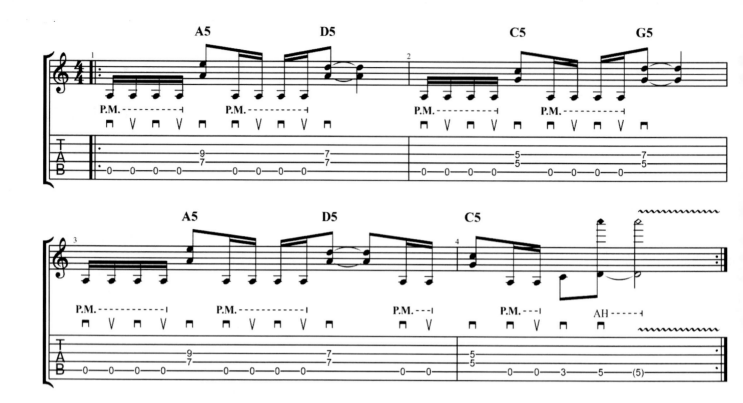

Returning to the key of G Minor and building on examples 1b and 1f, a new version includes 1/8th and 1/16th note pedalling on the low E string.

Example 1k:

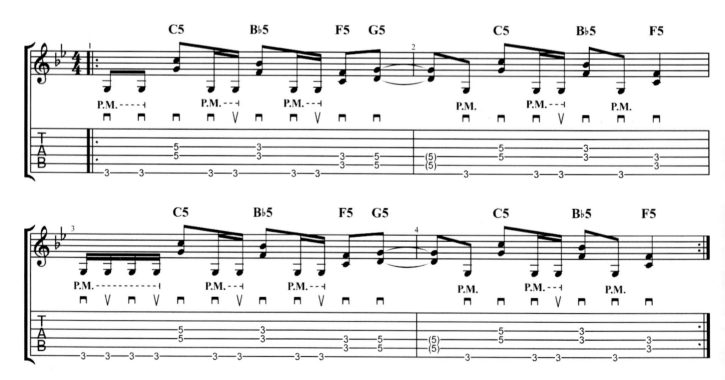

Based on the B Minor Pentatonic scale, the next riff uses all 1/16th notes for the bass note pedalling.

Since each chord after the first inverted power chord is struck with an upstroke, keep good timing and avoid string noise as you move between the bass note and chord stabs.

Example 1l:

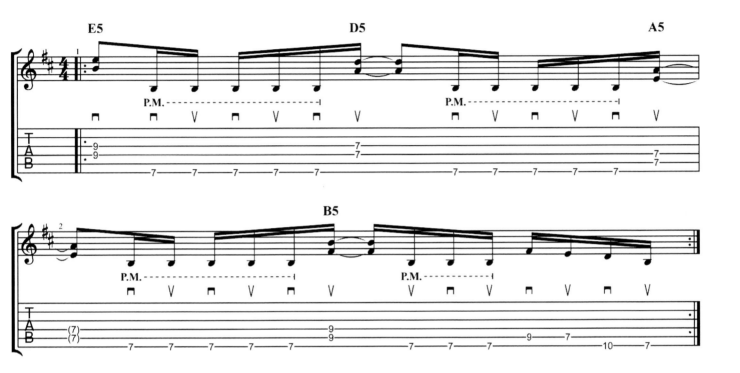

Next up, we're going to add one extra note to the pentatonic scale using a major 2nd or 9th.

Bar one of this Zakk Wylde (Ozzy Osbourne) style riff goes from the bottom to the top of the pentatonic box to include a double-stop on the B and high E strings. These two notes (E and A) provide the minor 7th and the minor 3rd of an F# minor chord.

In bar two, beat 2, the added G# note allows us to sneak an E major chord fragment into the riff.

We'll look more at chord fragmentation in Chapter Three.

Example 1m:

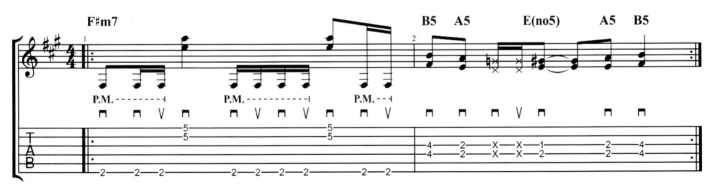

One of the biggest rock albums in 1984 was Van Halen's album of the same name, *1984*. Emulating the classic *Hot for Teacher* track from that album, the next riff is played over a fast shuffle at 230bpm.

I draw on the A Minor Blues scale for this riff, not only for the scale run in bar one, but also for the 8th fret power chord in bar two. The 5th of this chord, on the 8th fret of the D string, does not belong to the scale, but it fits nicely between the other inverted power chords – an idea Eddie Van Halen often used.

Example 1n:

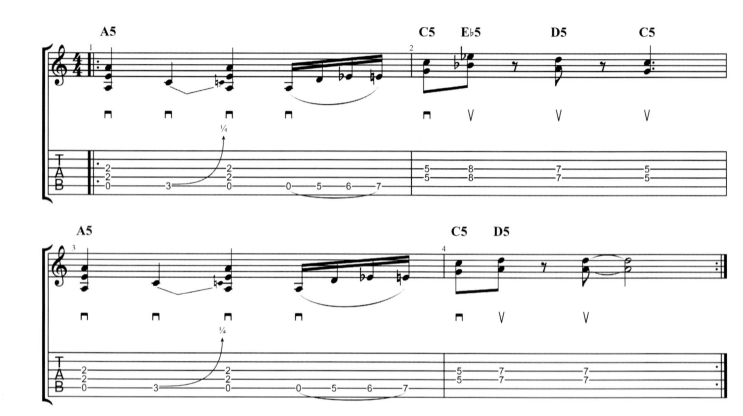

Completing this chapter is a riff that takes influence from *Paradise City* (Guns N' Roses) and *Monkey Business* (Skid Row), using 1/16th notes to move through inverted power chords faster than previous examples.

Since the bassline on the audio outlines the F#, B, and A notes in bar one, I'm not thinking about all the passing inverted power chords as significant changes to the harmony, but rather ways of creating movement around the highlighted chords indicated above the notation.

Bar one includes a passing tone chord on the 3rd fret of the A and D strings. It works because the 5th string C natural note is part of the minor blues scale.

Example 1o:

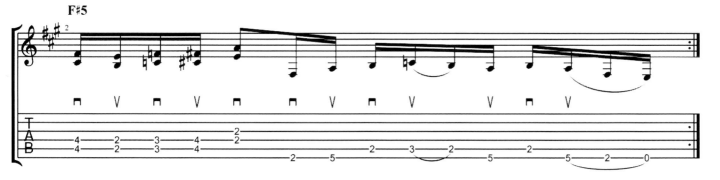

Now that you've worked through each of the "boxed" ideas from this chapter, try writing your own riffs based on the pentatonic format. In the audio download, you'll find two bonus jam tracks featuring drums and bass. Use these tracks to borrow, steal, and transform ideas from this chapter to create your own riffs.

In the next chapter, you'll learn to create chord progressions in any key without a theory degree.

Suggested listening related to this chapter by artist, track and guitarist(s):

- Rainbow – *All Night Long* (Ritchie Blackmore)

- Mötley Crüe – *Live Wire* (Mick Mars)

- Van Halen – *Hot for Teacher* (Edward Van Halen)

- Europe – *Dance the Night Away* (John Norum)

- Judas Priest – *Turbo Lover* (Glenn Tipton, KK Downing)

- Vixen – *Edge of a Broken Heart* (Jan Kuehnemund)

- TNT – *Everyone's a Star* (Ronni LeTekro)

- Guns N' Roses – *Paradise City* (Slash, Izzy Stradlin)

- Skid Row – *Youth Gone Wild* (Dave Sabo, Scotty Hill)

- Ozzy Osbourne – *Miracle Man* (Zakk Wylde)

Chapter Two: The Big Chorus

While we guitar players love to set the scene for a song with a great riff, sometimes we just need to deliver some big chord progressions and let the vocal melodies take centre stage.

So, before we cover the next steps of riff writing, let's have a quick run through diatonic harmony – the chords that belong to major and minor keys. This information will help you to write progressions that belong to a specific key and show you how to jump across to other keys and borrow chords from those.

Besides this overview, you can study theory basics in Joseph Alexander's book, *The Practical Guide to Modern Music Theory for Guitarists*.

Let's begin by looking at the chords that belong to the key of C Major. This key has no sharps or flats, so it will be easy to see if we come across a chord that doesn't belong to the key.

The notes in the C Major scale are C, D, E, F, G, A, B, and back to C.

That construction can be memorised as…

Tone, tone, semitone, tone, tone, tone, semitone

… which describes the interval or distance between each note (tone = whole step, and semitone = half step if you're used to US terminology).

Triads (our basic chordal unit) are formed by stacking the notes of the scale on top of each other in 3rds. They are so-called because they contain three separate notes (even when we expand them into different octaves to create bigger shapes).

Stacking diatonic 3rds using the C Major scale results in the following triads:

1. C major: C, E, G

2. D minor: D, F, A

3. E minor: E, G, B

4. F major: F, A, C

5. G major: G, B, D

6. A minor: A, C, E

7. B diminished: B, D, F

Notice that the "harmonised" scale comprises major, minor, and diminished triads and uses only the notes of the scale. Alter any of these notes or use the wrong chord type, and you'll end up in another key or simply out of key. If you need proof, replace all the chords above with major triads and enjoy the horror!

We can remember the harmonic progression of any major key as…

Major, minor, minor, major, major, minor, diminished.

Here they are in order with root notes along the A string. In case you're wondering, each of these diatonic triads are voiced with four notes, as the root note of each chord is doubled up.

Example 2a:

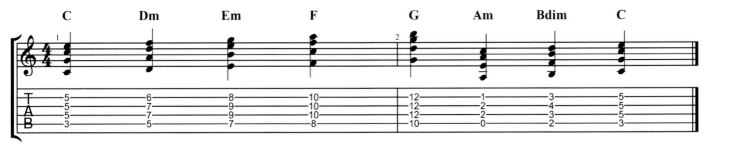

Let's switch to the key of G Major and do the same thing. The notes in the G Major scale are G, A, B, C, D, E, F#, and G. The diatonic triads now look like this, with some of the chords having root notes on the low E string.

Example 2b:

For reference, here are the triads mapped out in *all* keys. A major key can also be approached from its relative minor key i.e. the chords in the key of C Major are the same as those in A Minor. We're just focusing on a different tonal centre. Below, each row shows the name of the major key first, then its relative minor key.

For completeness, I've included every key, but some overlap as they contain the same pitches but different spellings. E.g. the notes of the B Major scale are enharmonically the same as those in Cb Major. The keys of F# Major and Gb Major are also enharmonic equivalents.

Key	I	II	III	IV	V	VI	VII
C / Am	C major	D minor	E minor	F major	G major	A minor	B dim.
G / Em	G major	A minor	B minor	C major	D major	E minor	F# dim.
D / Bm	D major	E minor	F# minor	G major	A major	B minor	C# dim.
A / F#m	A major	B minor	C# minor	D major	E major	F# minor	G# dim.
E / C#m	E major	F# minor	G# minor	A major	B major	C# minor	D# dim.
B / G#m	B major	C# minor	D# minor	E major	F# major	G# minor	A# dim.
Cb / Abm	Cb major	Db minor	Eb minor	Fb major	Gb major	Ab minor	B dim.
F# / D#m	F# major	G# minor	A# minor	B major	C# major	D# minor	E# dim.
Gb / Ebm	Gb major	Ab minor	Bb minor	Cb major	Db major	Eb minor	F dim.
Db / Bbm	Db major	Eb minor	F minor	Gb major	Ab major	Bb minor	C dim.
Ab / Fm	Ab major	Bb minor	C minor	Db major	Eb major	F minor	G dim.
Eb / Cm	Eb major	F minor	G minor	Ab major	Bb major	C minor	D dim.
Bb / Gm	Bb major	C minor	D minor	Eb major	F major	G minor	A dim.
F / Dm	F major	G minor	A minor	Bb major	C major	D minor	E dim.

You can use the above table as a quick reference when writing chord progressions, but another useful tool is the Circle of Fifths diagram.

This shows how keys move clockwise in perfect 5ths or anticlockwise in perfect 4ths. If you want to change key or borrow a chord from another key, using a neighbouring key will usually work well.

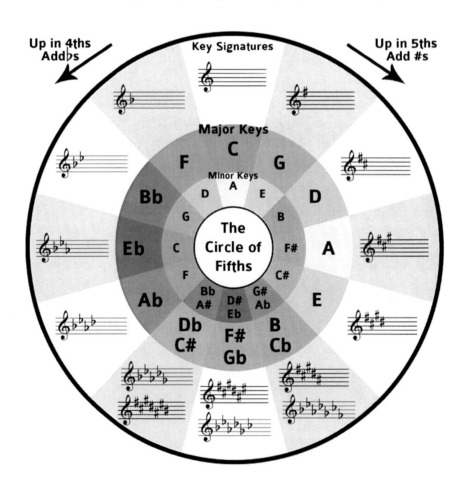

Creating Rock Chord Progressions

Now that we have some basic theory, let's talk about common chord progressions in '80s rock.

Stringing together any selection of chords from the rows in the previous table will give us a progression in that key, but many of the big rock hits we know and love used four chords more than the others.

Notice that each chord in the table is assigned a Roman numeral that describes its position in the key. This is a useful musical shorthand, which means we can describe a chord progression in *any* key just by referring to the Roman numerals.

Chords I, IV, V, and VI, have provided us with many radio anthems and stadium classics. Let's take a look at some different configurations of these chords.

The I, V, VI, IV progression is still used in a lot of pop hits today. In the '80s, it was the vehicle for anthemic choruses like *Take on Me* (A-ha), *Don't Stop Believin'* (Journey), *I Remember You* (Skid Row), *Walk Away* (Dokken), *Superstitious* (Europe), and *With or Without You* (U2).

Using the previous table, you can play the progression in any key by matching the row of your key choice with the Roman numerals at the top. Hence, a I, V, VI, IV progression in the key of E Major uses the chords E major, B major, C# minor, and A major.

With some embellishments, here's a rhythm part perfect for a slow rock track or a power ballad.

Example 2c:

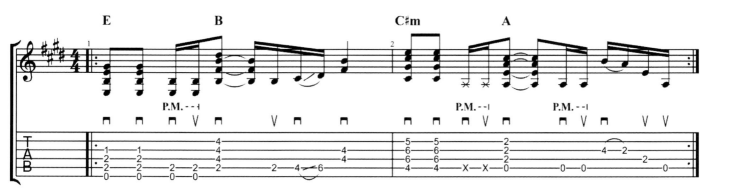

Stretching out the changes to one chord per bar, here's the same progression in the key of D Major. I added some suspended 4ths and 2nds to decorate the chords on beat 4 of bars one to three.

Example 2d:

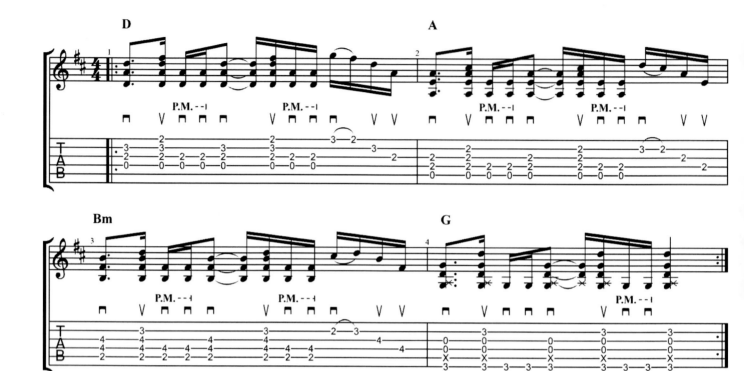

Another configuration of the same chords is the widely used VI, IV, I, V, which has been used to give us the chorus hooks of tunes like *Africa* by Toto, *Alone* by Heart, *Poison* by Alice Cooper, *Listen to Your Heart* by Roxette and *18 and Life* by Skid Row.

Hitmaking songwriters like Desmond Child and Dianne Warren have loved using this chord progression which, in the key of A Major, goes F# minor, D major, A major, and E major.

Example 2e:

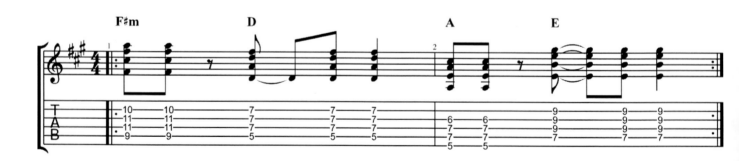

One more often-called-upon progression uses three chords: the VI, IV, and V. In the key of G Major, that's E minor, C major, and D major.

To make a riff from these chords, try pedalling the open E string and adding some small melodic fills.

As with most progressions in this chapter, any major or minor chord can be simplified to power chord form for a stripped-back sound. To do so here, exclude the notes on the B string in this example, which contains the 3rd interval of each chord.

Example 2f:

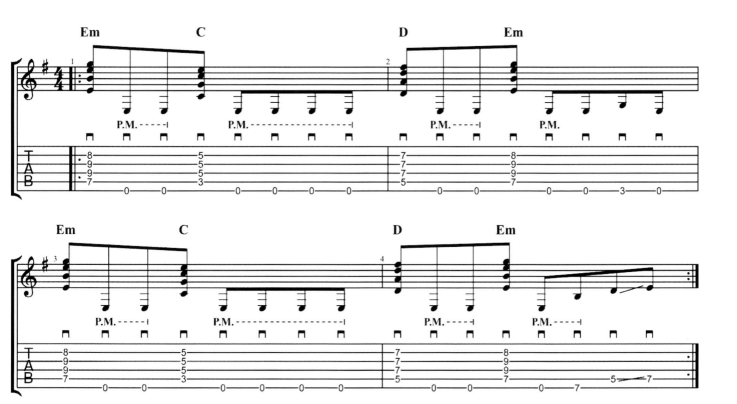

We'll get into scale-based riffs in detail in Chapter Six, but for now, try replacing some of the minor chords with minor pentatonic riff ideas.

Here's a reworking of the previous example, substituting the E minor triad in bars two and four with minor pentatonic motifs.

Example 2g:

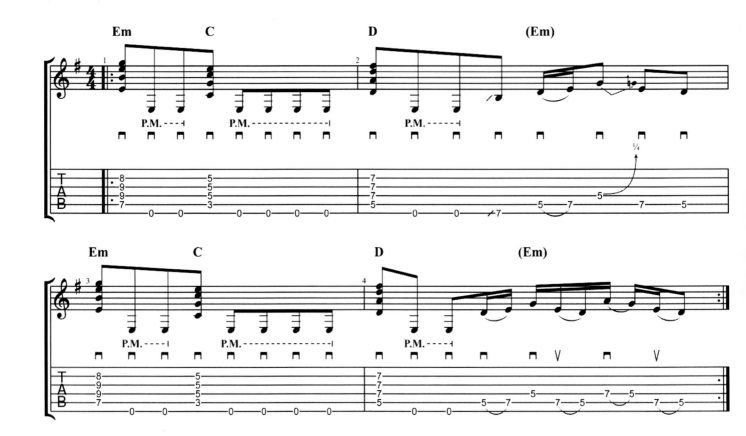

On the sleaze- and glam-rock side of things, the "big chorus" commonly relies less on minor chords and more on the three major chords in each key: the I, IV, and V chords.

Under the influence of AC/DC, Rose Tattoo, and perhaps even southern rock, bands like Guns N' Roses, Faster Pussycat, and Poison emphasised the fifth chord of the key, leaning into its Mixolydian tonality (perhaps unconsciously).

So, when playing the chords A major, G major, and D major, you might assume that the progression is in the key of A Major. However, studying the key chart at the beginning of the chapter, you'll see that those chords are the fifth, fourth, and first chords in the key of D Major – the only key that contains all three chords. It's just that the A major chord in this scenario feels like "home", rather than resolving to the I chord.

Here's a riff in the key of D Major using this scenario. To add a bluesy tinge, I bend into the C# note of the A major chord from a semitone below (C natural to C#) in bars one and four.

You can pick it all with downstrokes or insert upstrokes where it feels right.

Example 2h:

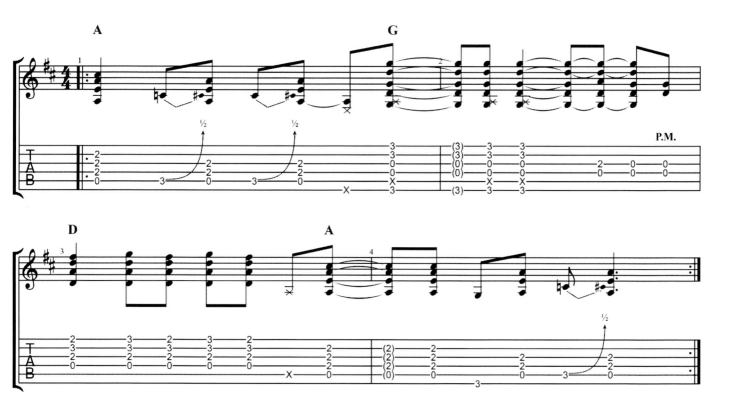

Here are the same chords in an AC/DC inspired riff, once again beginning with the V chord. For this one, try comparing playing all downstrokes to the alternate pick strokes indicated. Downstrokes are used for notes landing on a beat and upstrokes are used for the & of each beat.

Example 2i:

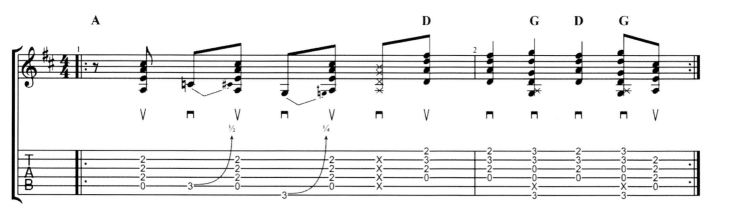

For some listening homework on treating the V chord as the tonal centre, try these tracks:

- Poison – *Nothing but a Good Time* (C.C. DeVille)

- Guns N' Roses – *Paradise City* (Slash, Izzy Stradlin)

- AC/DC – *Back in Black* (Angus and Malcolm Young)

- KISS – *Lick It Up* (Paul Stanley, Vinnie Vincent)

In the next section, we'll use chords from *outside* the parent key to enhance our progressions.

Modulating Progressions

When you know a little about how keys work, you can use that information to go into other keys for more chordal options.

In the next set of examples, I'll show you a few little tricks many rockers use to move into other keys for creative purposes.

Example 2j uses the chords E major, B major, D major, and A major.

Is it in the key of E Major?

Not exactly, as there's no D major chord in that key.

Is it in the key of A Major, then?

Well, there's no B major chord in that key.

How about the keys of D Major or B Major?

Nope, now two of the chords don't belong.

The way I think of this progression (which has an early Def Leppard vibe to my ears) is that bar one uses the I and V chords in the key of E Major, and bar two uses the I and V chords in the key of D Major.

In other words, the tonal centre *modulates* down a tone, then back again in bar three, modulating down again in bar four.

The pedalled low E string helps keep it all together as a consistent thread.

Example 2j:

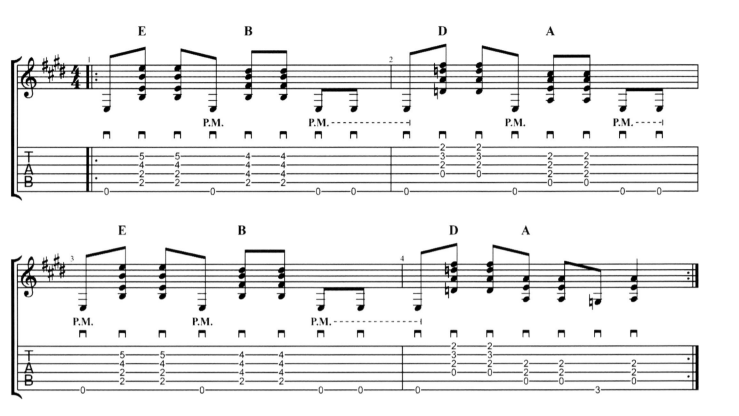

Let's take the moving I to V idea further and add in the key of C too, giving us a progression that draws on three keys: E major, D major, C major, and back to D major.

As with the previous example, pedalling the open low E string (ideally with the bassist playing an octave lower), creates excellent continuity across the key changes. Many listeners will think they're hearing one diatonic chord progression the whole time.

Example 2k:

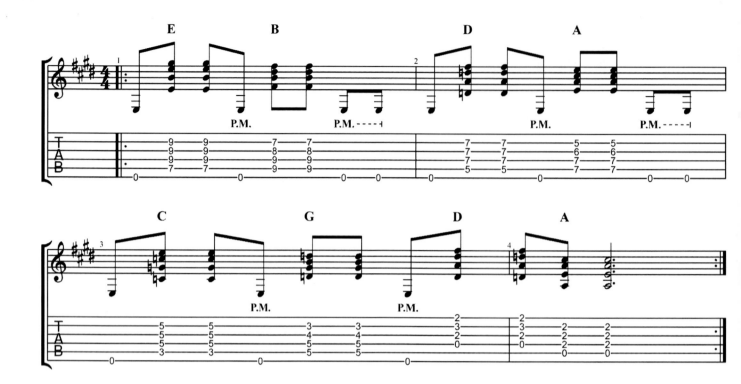

Alice Cooper's 1989 smash hit *Poison* is an excellent example of a progression that moves through multiple keys to create interest and avoid repetition.

Based on the VI, IV, I, V progression, the chorus of the song uses four separate keys: Bb Major (G Minor), Eb Major (C Minor), C Major (A Minor) and F Major (D Minor).

Look back at the Circle of Fifths diagram and you'll see that the first and second keys are neighbours, as are the third and fourth keys.

Example 2l uses the Alice Cooper key changes to inspire a progression in four keys: G Major, C Major, A Major, and D Major.

To keep it beefy sounding, I'm using power chords on the guitar in the audio, with keyboards playing the triads indicated.

See what other chord progressions you can extend by moving the key in fourths or fifths at a time.

Example 2l:

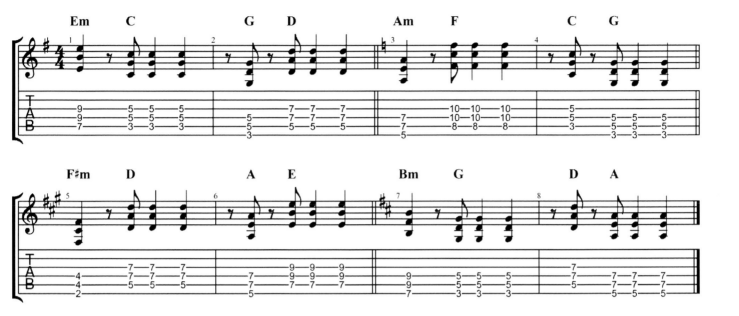

Pivot chords are a great way to change from one key to another. Since major and minor triads exist at multiple degrees of diatonic scales, we can use a chord that two keys have in common to move from one key to the other without it sounding jarring.

Iron Maiden's classic *Aces High* uses pivot chords to modulate from one minor key to another. In the following example, I'll use the same approach to move from the key of A Minor to C Minor.

The first four bars of this riff contain A minor, F major, and G major chords – all found in the key of A Minor.

The F major and G major triads can also be found in the harmonised key of C Melodic Minor (C, D, Eb, F, G, A, B), so in this example they act as pivot chords to help us move the whole progression smoothly up a minor 3rd. The G major chord in particular creates a perfect cadence into C minor.

Example 2m:

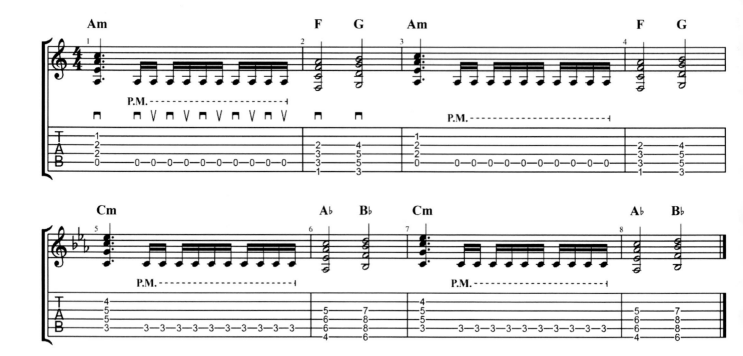

Up next is a riff that might be at home in the hands of Ratt's Warren DeMartini or Winger's Reb Beach.

Bars 1-2 are built around A major and G major triads with a pedalled A note on the fifth string. In isolation, these two bars create the impression of a riff in the key of D Major, using chords V and IV.

Since the G chord can also be the V chord in the key of C Major, I use this to pivot to the F major (chord IV in C Major), returning to the G chord in bars 3-4, and ending with a short walk down the C Major scale in bar four.

The resulting riff is an even mix of the keys of D Major and C Major using a common chord as a pivot point.

Example 2n:

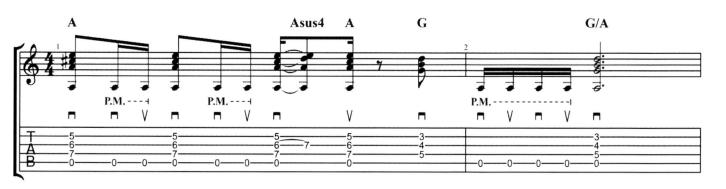

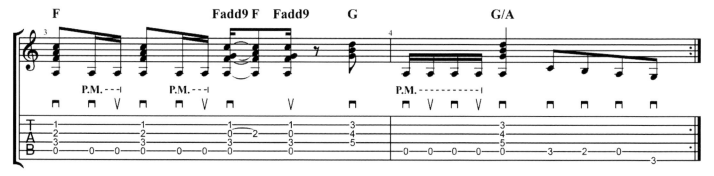

Tips for creating chord progressions for your songs:

• Memorise the sequence of chord types that occurs in major keys

• Learn common chord progressions and practice moving them to other keys (transposing)

• Analyse progressions you already know and determine their keys

• Experiment with moving to other keys using pivot chords, or transposing from key to key using the Circle of Fifths

In the next chapter, you'll learn the idea of *chord fragmentation:* exploring various chord shapes and using smaller fragments of them to create a wide range of riffing options.

Chapter Three: Fun Size Chord Fragments

Now that you know how progressions and keys work, it's time to get more creative in arranging chord-oriented riffing.

Chord fragmentation allows us to express the essence of the harmony in a cool way that can become a signature part of a song.

"Fun Size" is a marketing term coined by snack companies that offer smaller portions of their chocolate bars or treats. In this chapter, I'll take the same approach to chords, using fragments of open and barre chord shapes to create compact units for your riff catalogue.

As you apply the chord fragments in this chapter with pedal tones, rhythmic motifs, and progressions, you'll begin to hear the secret sauce behind your favourite '80s MTV hits by Van Halen, Ratt, Autograph, Def Leppard, and Winger, as well as the minor tonality riffs of Michael Schenker, Yngwie Malmsteen, John Norum, and the more metallic side of '80s rock.

Let's start by looking at chords as fretboard-encompassing entities, then breaking them into clusters to use in riffs.

Major Chord Fragmentation

Using the common CAGED chords, here are fretboard maps for C major, A major, G major, E major, and D major triads.

Pretty soon, you'll notice how each major chord uses the same set of shapes, starting from a different point each time. All other major chords can be found by moving these patterns up or down the required frets.

Figure 3a: C Major

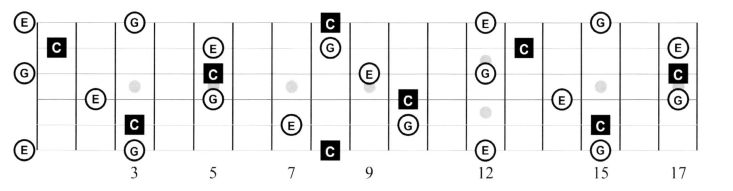

Figure 3b: A Major

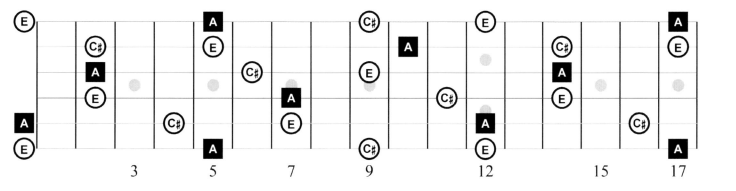

Figure 3c: G Major

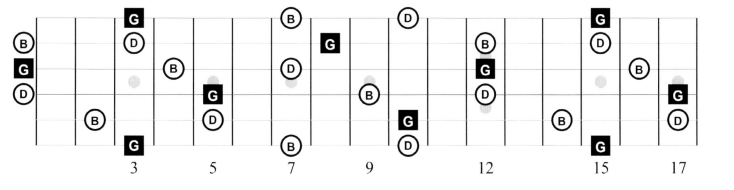

Figure 3d: E Major

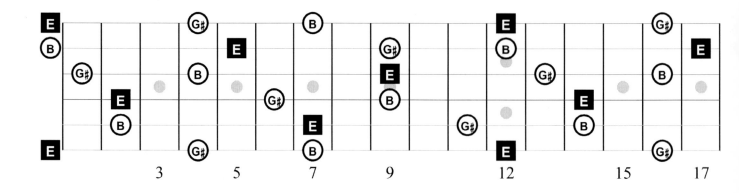

Figure 3e: D Major

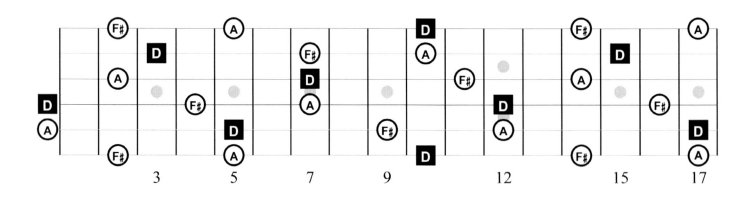

Fretboard maps can be overwhelming at first sight, but they become more manageable when we break each chord into clusters that move up and down smaller groups of strings, such as three-string groupings.

Here, for example, are some A major triad fragments arranged on the D, G, and B strings, then the A, D, and G strings.

Example 3a:

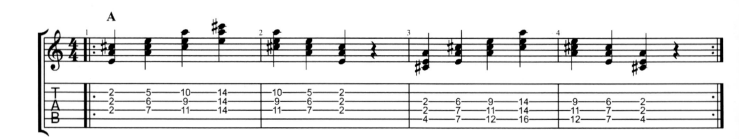

Adhering to the fretboard maps, try the previous exercise using the remaining CAGED chords, starting in the lowest position and moving up. Here's the drill with a D Major chord to get you started with the rest.

Example 3b:

By knowing the shapes of each CAGED chord on the same groups of strings, you'll be able to connect chords in a voice-leading manner rather than jumping around the fretboard.

Here's an exercise that uses fragments of five major chords, each new one beginning close to where the previous chord finished. This process can be done on every string group to improve chord knowledge.

Example 3c:

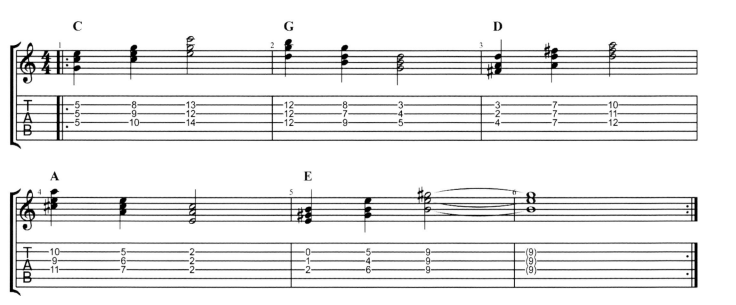

Things start to sound more like '80s radio when we add some rhythm, and a pedalled bass note, and blur the lines of diatonic harmony as we borrow chords from major and minor keys.

Example 3d uses a muted open A string to provide the pulse, while the chord fragments borrow from parallel keys that share the A note.

A simple way to think about the progression is as a IV to I cadence that moves through the keys of D Major (bar one), A Major (bar two), C Major (bar three) and G Major (end of bar three and into bar four).

Example 3d:

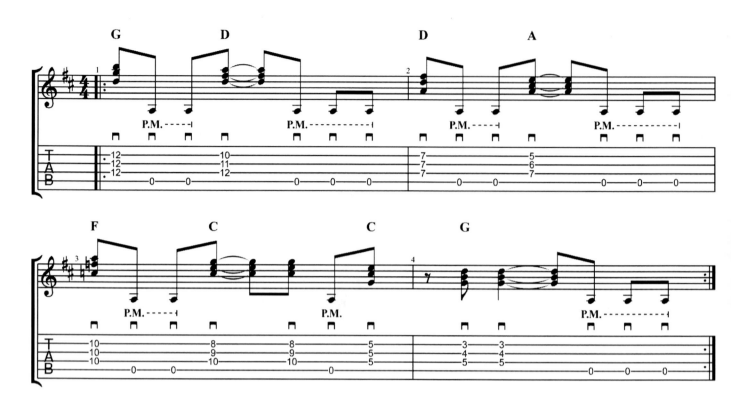

Here's another demonstration of riffing through a few different keys, using a pedalled bass note to tie things together. This time, the low E string is pumped in between chord fragments.

Example 3e:

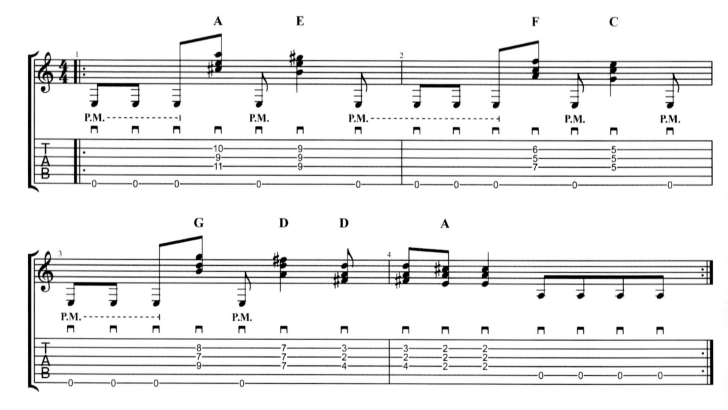

Featuring diatonic chord fragmentation and some busier pedal note picking, here's a riff in the key of A Major, styled on the Ozzy Osbourne classic *Crazy Train* (featuring the late, great Randy Rhoads).

The voice leading creates smooth transitions between the A major, E major, and D major chord fragments. Bar four ends with a short descending phrase from the A Major scale.

Example 3f:

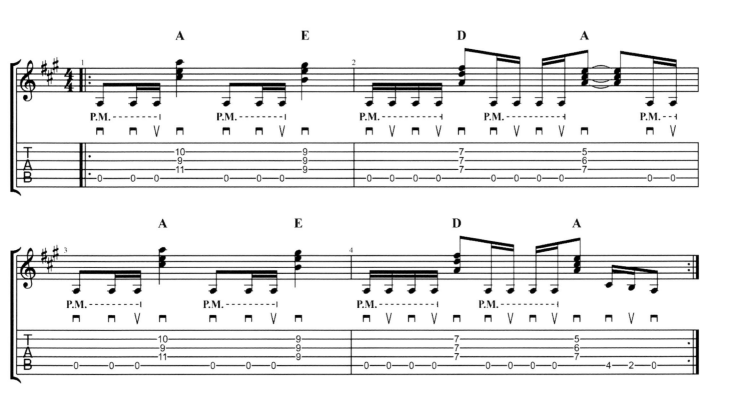

A common attribute of Edward Van Halen's rhythm guitar approach was to add suspended 4ths to major chords. Arpeggiating was another regular go-to in his style.

Using the I, V, and IV chords from the key of E Major, this riff conjures up the vibe of Van Halen's *Dance the Night Away* (not the Europe track mentioned in Chapter One).

Example 3g:

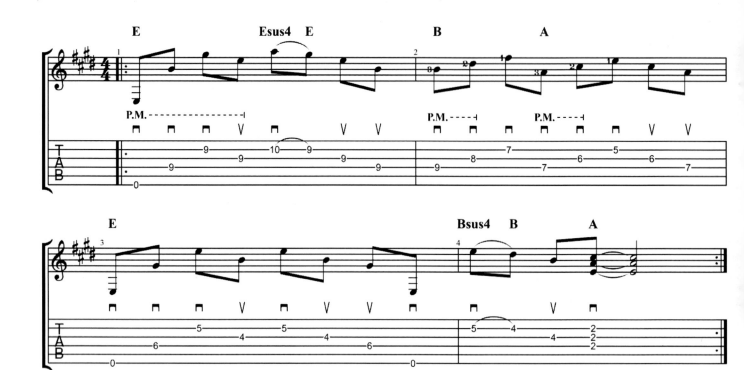

While Swedish guitarist Yngwie Malmsteen is mainly known for his neoclassical shred style, the '80s saw Malmsteen trying his hand at commercial success with tracks like *Heaven Tonight* from the *Odyssey* album.

Doubled by keyboards for a very slick sound, Example 3h emulates Malmsteen's style at the time, taking A-shaped barre chord fragments and adding 4ths and 5ths as melody notes on the B string.

While the riff begins and resolves on an E major chord, the C major and D major chords are borrowed from the key of E Minor.

Example 3h:

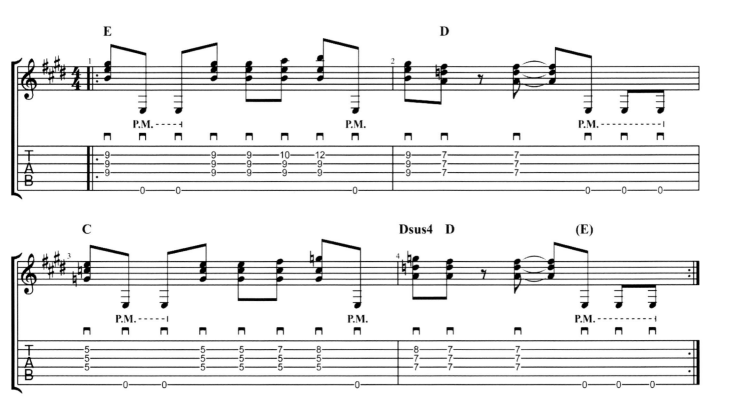

Your pedal tone can impact the overall tonality that the listener perceives, even with the same moving chords.

Here's a riff in the style of Neal Schon, inspired by the Journey song, *Escape*.

In the first four bars of the riff, E major, B major, and A major chords are played in between an E root note. This is an undeniable E Ionian sound, as we pedal the E note between the primary chords of E Major.

Using the same chord parts, we can allude to an A Lydian sound (the fourth mode of the E Major scale) by using an A pedal tone. The bass guitar in the audio duplicates the change of bass notes.

Three melody notes at the end of bars four and eight let the listener know something different is coming.

Listen to the audio and note how the bass notes change your perception of the same chord fragments.

Example 3i:

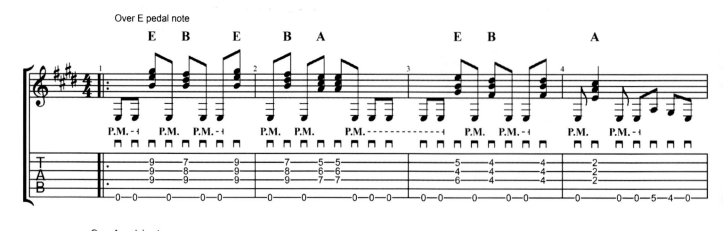

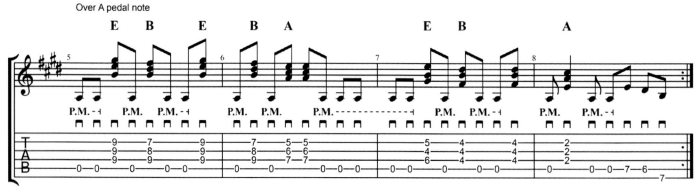

The next section will look at minor chord fragmentation to get darker sounds and expand our diatonic options.

Suggested listening related to this section:

- Van Halen – *Unchained, Panama* (Edward Van Halen)

- Def Leppard – *Photograph* (Steve Clark and Phil Collen)

- Yngwie Malmsteen – *Heaven Tonight, Fire*

- Autograph – *Turn up the Radio* (Steve Lynch)

- *White Lion* – Little Fighter (Vito Bratta)

- *Bon Jovi* – Let It Rock (Richie Sambora)

- TNT – *10,000 Lovers, Listen To Your Heart* (Ronni Le Tekro)

- Journey – *Escape* (Neal Schon)

- Winger – *Seventeen* (Reb Beach)

Minor Chord Fragmentation

It's time to map out some minor chords and apply those fragments to rhythm playing. Here are the layouts for E minor, A minor and D minor triads, since those are the most used minor chords in the open position.

Figure 3f: E Minor

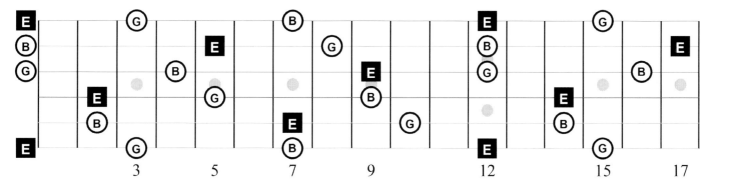

Figure 3g: A Minor

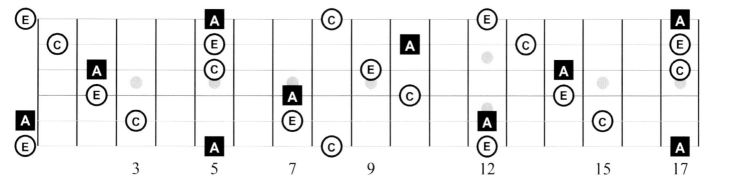

Figure 3h: D Minor

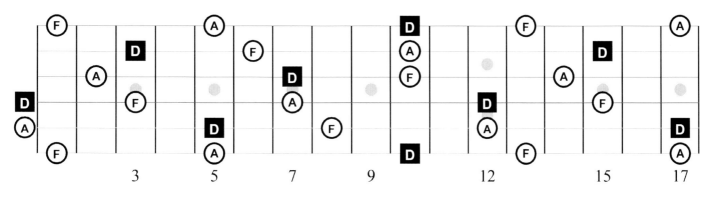

You can break these up into various string groups too, so here are two riff-drills to start.

Example 3j:

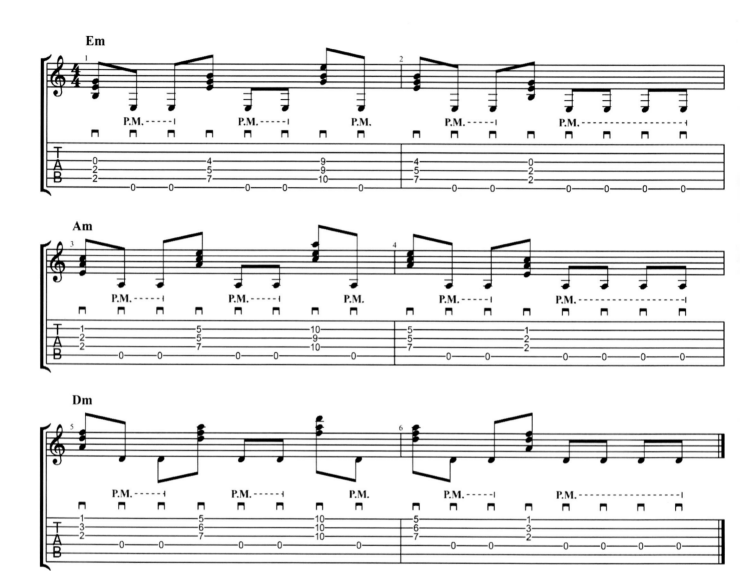

Example 3k:

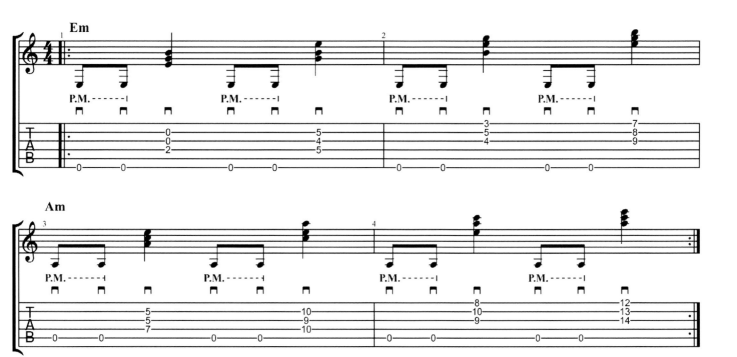

While the Sunset Strip bands were partying at the Rainbow Bar and Grill, countless bands on the European continent were forging identities of their own, inspired by Deep Purple, Led Zeppelin, UFO, and the NWOBHM (new wave of British heavy metal) bands like Iron Maiden, Saxon, Judas Priest, Angelwitch and Diamond Head.

Germany and Sweden became hotspots for the rise of melodic rock and metal, as bands like Scorpions and Accept reached full force, and newer acts like Europe, Yngwie Malmsteen, and Helloween took their spots on the international stage.

The scenes in England, Germany, and Sweden (to name three) have histories rich enough to deserve a book each, but to provide an overview, so you can create your own European-style riffs, we'll focus on the use of minor chords and keys for now.

While power chords can be shorthand for major or minor chords, many European guitarists used 3rd intervals liberally, incorporating root note and 3rd dyads into their power chord work.

Some of these moves would make it back to the USA and show up in the Bay Area thrash sound.

Example 3l:

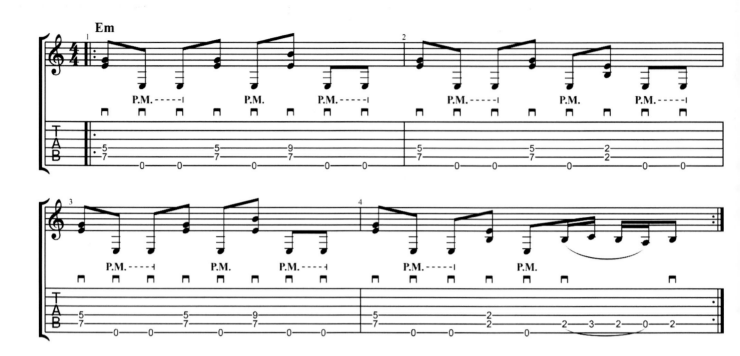

Guitarists like Michael Schenker (Scorpions, UFO, MSG) used root/3rd dyads from major and minor chords within the key to create rhythm parts.

Here's a riff in the Schenker style using such fragments from the key of E Minor over a pedalled low E note. There are no 5ths in any of the voicings.

Example 3m:

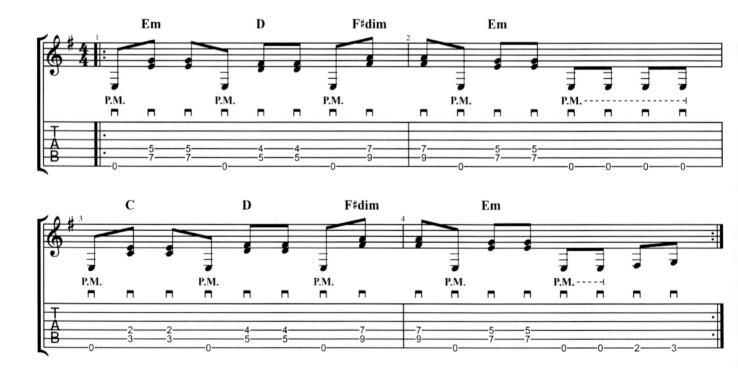

Taking influence from the Schenker approach, Yngwie Malmsteen tracks like *Demon Driver, Motherless Child* and *Crystal Ball* all featured two-string chord fragments with pedalled open string notes, as does the Europe classic *Wings of Tomorrow.*

As guitarists started speeding up their ideas, riffs veered into what would become known as Power Metal, demonstrated in this next riff.

Working this example up to and beyond 200bpm will be great for your picking hand as you switch between palm muting the low E string and accenting the chord fragments, almost exclusively with downstrokes.

Example 3n:

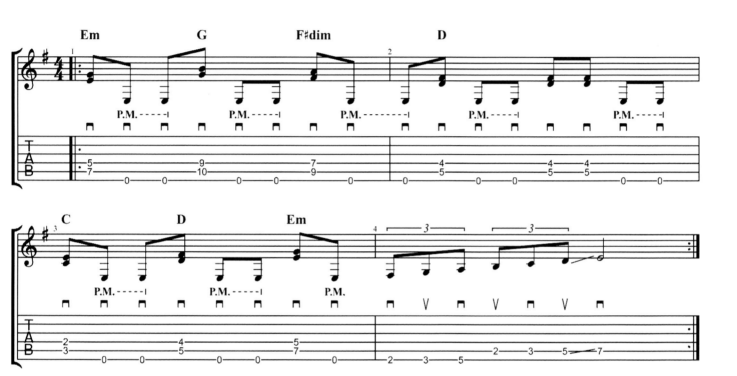

To create your own riffs in this style, refer to the chords and keys reference chart at the beginning of the chapter. Keys with open string root notes like E, A, and D, will be a great place to start with pedalled bass notes and diatonic dyads.

You can also challenge yourself to build a chord progression, then see what arrangement ideas you can embellish it with.

I'm going to start you off with the chord progression A minor, D minor, E major, A minor. These chords belong to the key of A Minor (the harmonic minor in the case of the E major chord).

I'll play the progression in a few ways using chord fragmentation and different rhythm approaches.

Example 3o is played in 12/8 time, which feels like 4/4 with constant 1/8th note triplets where accenting and chord placement are concerned.

Example 3o:

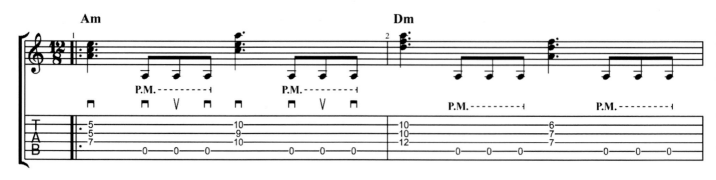

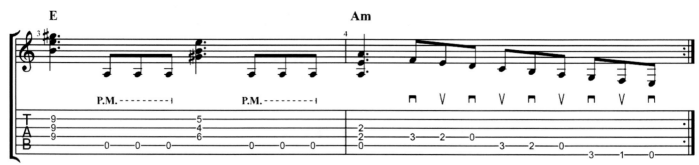

Changing styles, the next version starts with two-string A minor triad fragments in bar one. Then, over the D minor chord in bar two, I include a passing E minor triad fragment on beat 3.

Bar three is relatively straightforward with the low E string and two three-string fragments, while bar four takes some pentatonic inspiration from Chapter One of the book.

Example 3p:

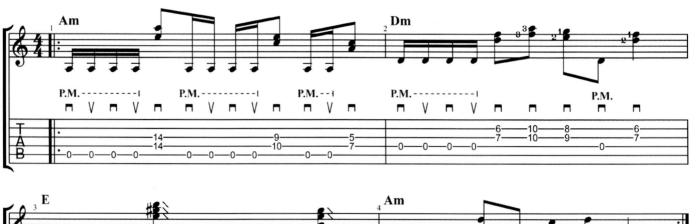

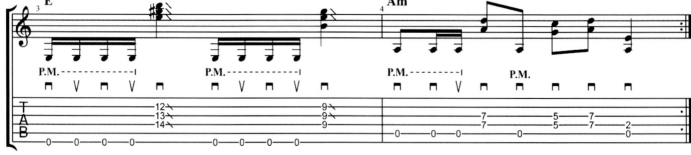

For the final version of the same chord progression, I'm taking a mid-tempo approach and including some suspended chords to create motion.

Suspended 4th chords can resolve to major or minor triads, so you'll see a suspension used for each chord in the progression.

Example 3q:

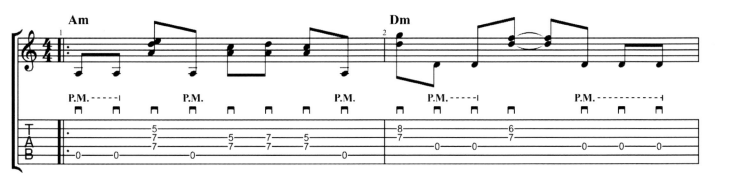

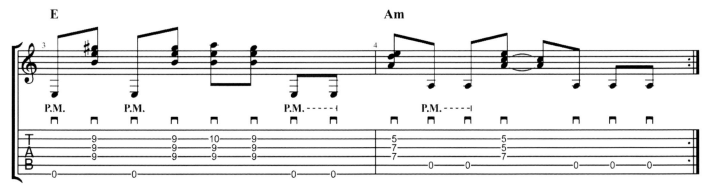

Chapter Four will focus on picking hand rhythm chops and fretting hand control.

Suggested listening for this section:

- Michael Schenker Group – *Desert Song*

- Yngwie Malmsteen – *Crystal Ball, Demon Driver*

- Metallica – *Orion* (James Hetfield, Kirk Hammett)

- Dokken – *So Many Tears* (George Lynch)

- Europe – *Wings of Tomorrow* (John Norum)

- Bon Jovi – *Wanted Dead or Alive* (Richie Sambora)

Chapter Four: Hone Your Rhythm Chops

In this chapter, I'll give you more work to practice your picking hand dexterity and fretting hand control.

Stylistically, we'll approach these chops with various riffs from metal gallops to shuffle grooves to funk-rock.

As you progress, you'll better understand what written rhythms will sound like, which pick strokes to use, and how to practice developing speed.

Let's begin with counting.

When there are a stream of 1/16th notes in a bar, you'll often hear the rhythm described as...

"1e&a, 2e&a, 3e&a, 4e&a"

...spoken as, "one ee and ah, two ee and ah" etc.

When playing this rhythm, create a picking motion that is smart and efficient, with downstrokes and upstrokes moving along one line of motion. Aim your downstrokes straight at the E string, towards the A string, and back along the same path.

Example 4a:

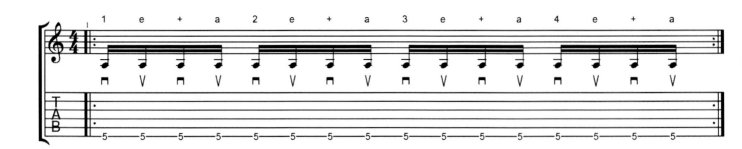

Gallop rhythms, which combine 1/8th and 1/16th notes, are counted aloud using just the relevant portions of the straight 1/16th rhythm.

So, Example 4b can be expressed as...

"one- and ah, two- and ah", etc., (written 1 &a, 2 &a, 3 &a, 4 &a)

...since there is no "ee" articulated in any of the beats.

A liberal amount of palm muting will make the notes below sound tight and controlled. Lightening the mute pressure allows more sustain. Since heavy palm muting creates a very staccato effect, muting this gallop will make it sound like there's a 1/16th note rest after the first note of each beat.

With two downstrokes in a row, don't delay bringing the pick back around the low E string after the first downstroke of each beat.

Example 4b:

Then we have a reverse gallop in Example 4c. Here, the 1/16th notes come first. This is counted,

"1e&, 2e&, 3e&, 4e&" or,

"one ee and, two ee and" etc.

It is picked down, up, down, repeatedly.

Example 4c:

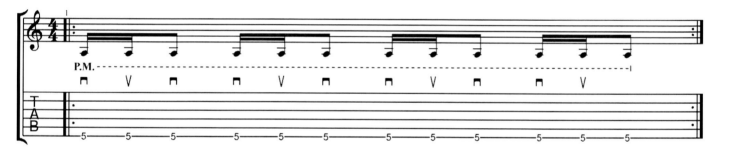

Adding chord fragments between fast, picked bass notes will likely produce a noticeable wrist flick at speed. This is fine and occurs in my picking every time I move between chord portions.

Here's a drill that moves between fragments of A minor and G major barre chords. I hold each shape down across six strings, using my picking hand to attack the required strings, with palm muting to control the sound and thwart any potential noise.

Example 4d:

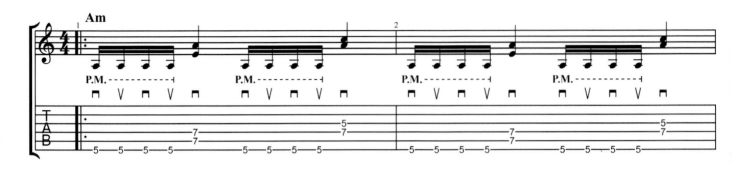

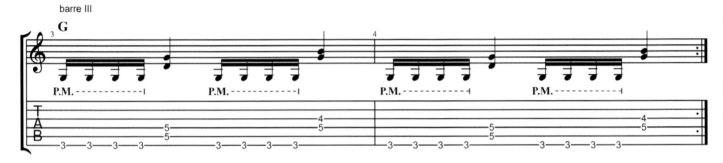

Let's include some fifth-string barre chords on the next run-through:

Example 4e:

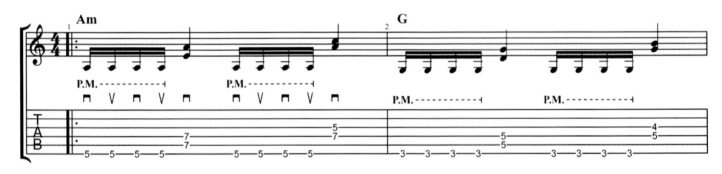

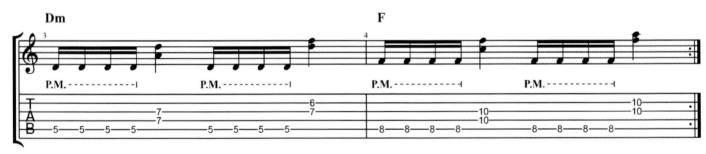

Gallop rhythms were a staple of '80s rock and metal, from the slow plod of Dio's *Holy Diver* (92bpm), the mid-tempo bounce of Europe's worldwide smash, *The Final Countdown* (118bpm), to the high energy pace of countless Iron Maiden songs (*The Trooper* was recorded at a spritely 160bpm).

When galloping with power chords at slower speeds, two or three strings in each pick stroke is feasible, as this Europe-style riff demonstrates.

Example 4f:

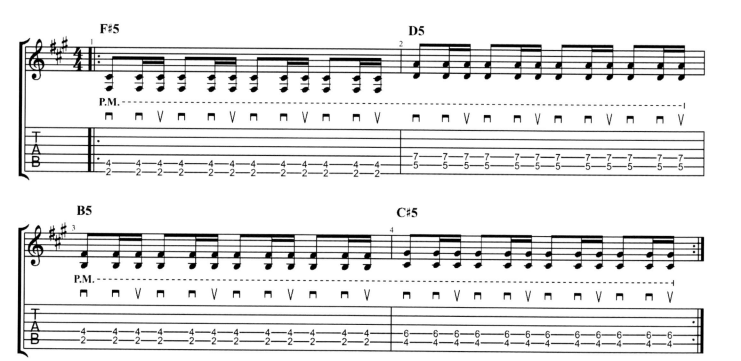

For the fast stuff, however, it's common to hear many European-style metal bands breaking up chords between the root note and upper notes, muting the former and punctuating the latter with snappy, open-sounding downstrokes.

Played in the key of G Minor, this riff is designed to get you pushing the tempo on galloping rhythms, alternating between 1/8th downstroke chord hits and 1/16th note muted alternate picking.

On the audio, I push this example up to 180bpm, but until you get there, ensure that your picking is rhythmically tight.

For fretting, use the index finger to press down the A string notes and mute the unused strings to keep everything tidy. You need enough contact to stop any sympathetic ringing on those strings.

Example 4g:

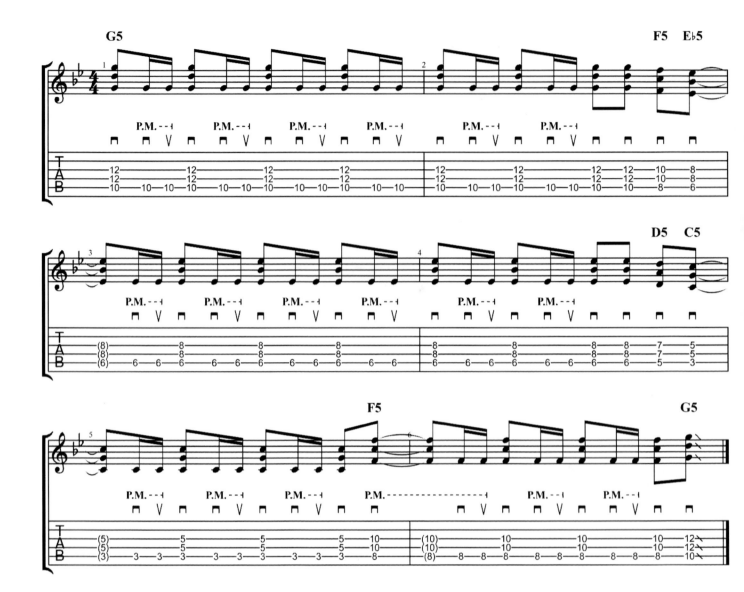

As the driving picking patterns of Euro-metal made their way over to the USA, the emergence of Metallica and Slayer took the influences of Black Sabbath and the NWOBHM and fused them into an exciting new direction that would be labelled *Thrash Metal*.

The reverse gallop was a common rhythm in the thrash genre. Slayer's *Raining Blood* is a classic example to check out. Even if the more metallic side of the '80s is not your cup of tea, this kind of rhythm at a high tempo is an excellent workout for picking hand development and control.

Here are two riffs designed to be played fast, mixing the reverse gallop with some 1/8th note down-picking in the styles of Metallica's James Hetfield and Slayer's Jeff Hanneman.

Regarding note choice, diatonic harmony frequently goes out of the window in thrash metal, creating a more sinister sound with deliberate chromaticism.

Example 4h:

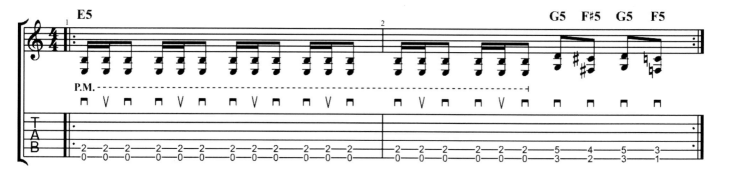

Example 4i:

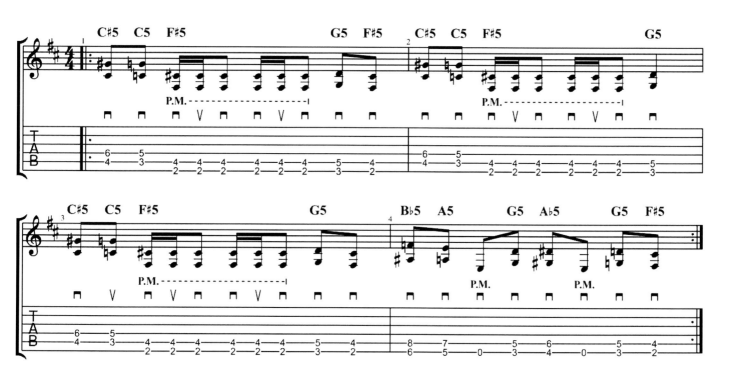

Incorporating 1/16th note triplets (sextuplets) into the tremolo picking segments, Example 4j syncs up with double kick drum work on the audio in the style of Metallica's *One*.

Example 4j:

Scale sequences are also valuable for increasing your picking chops for rhythm playing. Chapter Six focuses on the scale side of riffing, but let's do some prep now with ascending and descending sequences.

Example 4k goes up the A Natural Minor scale in bar one, descending in bar two. Each direction uses steps of four notes to move through the scale.

Example 4k:

Example 4l takes *fours* up and down the minor pentatonic scale, resulting in frequent string changing.

Example 4l:

As Aerosmith's second run in the late '80s gained momentum, many bands started incorporating more shuffle grooves into their hard rock riffs.

To work on 1/8th note shuffles, we can take the notes from the previous exercise and change the rhythmic approach.

As you'll see in the performance indicator, shuffled 1/8th notes are played with a triplet feel, where the notes that fall on the beat are worth two triplets and the notes in between are worth one triplet.

Be sure to play along and lock into the audio performance, which takes place over a half-time shuffle beat. You can play the notes muted, unmuted, or with both.

Example 4m:

Applying shuffled 1/8th notes to a riff, here's a groove inspired by late '80s Ratt and Aerosmith.

It's based on the E Minor Blues scale. Played with a half-time feel at 180bpm, the challenge is to stay locked into the beat while applying hammer-ons and pull-offs.

Example 4n:

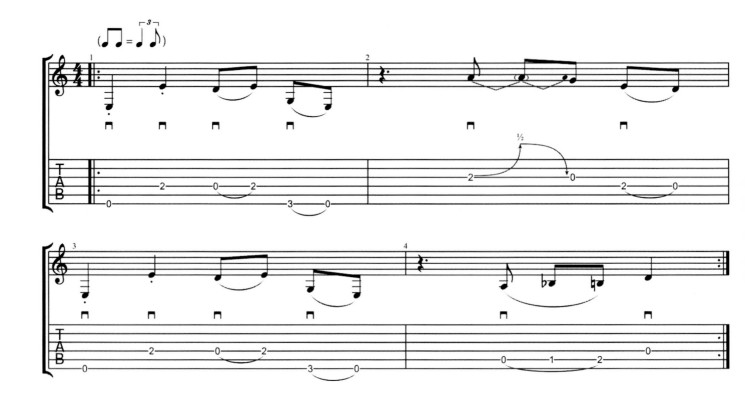

Start adding percussive pick strokes to take your groove further into pro territory.

Percussive pick strokes fill the space between chord hits in the next riff, centred around an A Mixolydian/A Blues sound.

To really deaden the strings, I cover the strings with my fretting hand and palm-mute with the picking hand.

Example 4o:

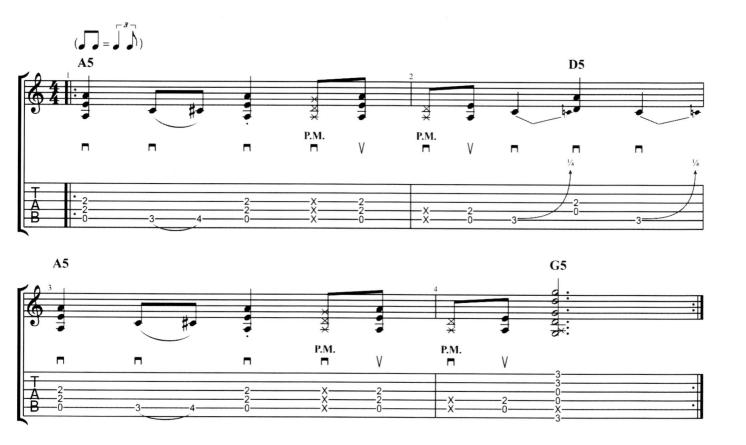

To finish the chapter, the final riff applies percussive pick strokes to a 1/16th note feel in the style of Slash (Guns N' Roses).

At the suggested tempo on the audio, muting is done with the fretting hand only. With lots of gain, it can get a little noisy, but Slash's style has quite a bit of that "rough around the edges" feel as a stylistic trait. So apply whatever level of detail you think will sound best.

Example 4p:

In the next chapter, we'll switch gears and get into some of those lush, clean chord parts heard in tracks by Def Leppard and Whitesnake.

Suggested listening related to this chapter:

- Dio – *Holy Diver* (Vivian Campbell)

- Europe – *Wasted Time, The Final Countdown* (John Norum)

- Iron Maiden – *The Trooper, Run To The Hills* (Dave Murray, Adrian Smith)

- Dokken – *Kiss of Death* (George Lynch)

- Metallica – *Battery, One* (James Hetfield, Kirk Hammett)

- Slayer – *Raining Blood* (Jeff Hanneman, Kerry King)

- Ratt – *Way Cool Jr* (Warren DeMartini, Robin Crosby)

- Guns N' Roses – *Welcome to the Jungle* (Slash, Izzy Stradlin)

- Ozzy Osbourne – *Bark at the Moon* (Jake E. Lee)

Chapter Five: Sparkly Clean Chord Parts

When it came to hit singles and radio airplay, power ballads and slow rock were defining aspects of rock repertoire in the '80s.

With radio being the number one way in which people heard new music, a hit song with airplay momentum could bring audiences to shows and introduce crowds to a band's more rocking tracks.

Hits like Whitesnake's *Is This Love* and Def Leppard's *Love Bites* reverberated with clean guitar parts, coated with stereo delay and chorus effects, setting the scene for the lead vocal.

In this chapter, I'll walk you through turning common chord progressions into radio-ready arrangements.

Let's start with tone.

To achieve the sounds heard in the audio for this chapter, you won't need a refrigerator-sized rackmount effects setup, just a nice clean tone, a modulation effect, and a time-based effect.

On my Kemper profiling amp, I start with the tone of a Marshall 1987x amp, with the drive almost all the way down.

I have a vintage chorus effect on the preamp-side of the effects (the "pedals" that would go in between the guitar and amp). This is probably styled on the Boss CE-2, but a contemporary chorus pedal will do just fine.

My setting for the chorus effect is with the rate and depth set halfway. The "rate" is how fast I want the modulation effect to cycle, and the "depth" is how wide I want the modulation. Dial these according to taste on the chorus that you have.

I have delay and reverb on the back end of the effects that come after the preamp (like an effects loop on a regular amp).

I want both the time-based effects to enhance the sound of the chords without bouncing back intrusively, so I have the "Legacy Delay" on the Kemper set to just a couple of repeats and an effect level of 50% of the original sound.

The Legacy Delay allows me to choose two speeds for the repeats, so I set one at 325 milliseconds and the other at 250ms. A single delay speed will be okay if that's what you have.

At the end of the effects chain, I have a Hall reverb with 2 seconds delay time. It's set higher in volume than the delay, with a mix level of 63%.

With this tone setup, I usually use the neck pickup on my guitars for a sound with chime and depth.

For the playing aspects of this chapter, I'll be avoiding deep music theory in favour of practical ways you can make creative parts out of chord progressions.

Creative Clean Parts

In this chapter, I'll take some basic chord progressions and develop them into exciting parts with some simple processes. Four devices I'll be using are:

- Arpeggiated chords

- Chord extensions

- Open string common tones

- Fretted common tones

The arpeggiating of chords allows each note to stand out and have an individual rhythmic placement. When layered over a strum or power chord hit from a second guitar, an arpeggiated part can add harmonic, melodic and rhythmic value to the song.

Common tones are notes shared between two or more chords. We can use pre-existing common tones or add new ones to tie an arrangement together nicely, rather than it sounding like block chords moving around in wide intervals.

Let's start with a simple chord progression consisting of E minor, C major, and D major chords in the key of E Minor. Played over a slow, 1/8th note bassline, the arpeggiated chords sound *okay* but not remarkable.

Example 5a:

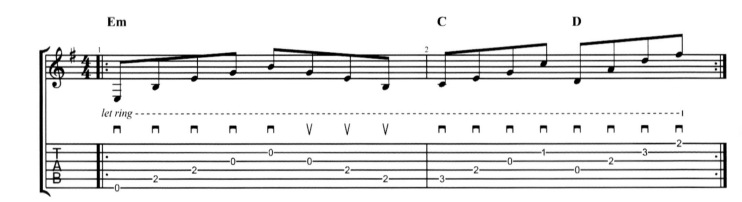

The first thing I'll do to dress up the progression is to embellish the E minor chord with some extensions, instead of repeating the three triad notes in different octaves.

Example 5b now has an F# note on the D string (4th fret) and a D note on the B string (3rd fret), making the new chord Emin9. It's a richer sound already.

Example 5b:

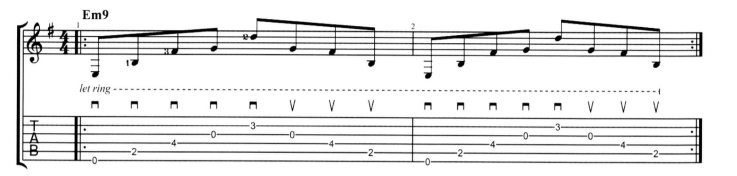

Next, I'll replace the open chord C major and D major shapes with voicings that include some notes from the Emin9 chord. This will provide excellent continuity.

Bar two of Example 5c uses C and D root notes with part of the Emin9 chord shape. The resulting chords have longer (and more convoluted) names, but the progression flows better with some common threads.

Cadd9add#11 retains the notes C and G from a C major triad, and Dadd11 keeps the notes D and F# from a D major triad.

MTV, here we come!

Example 5c:

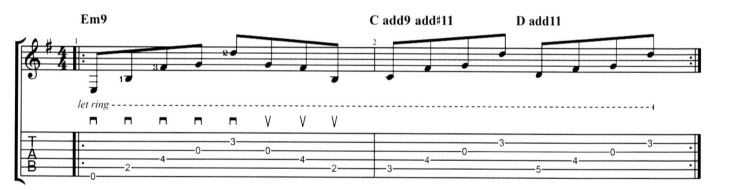

That was a good idea, but let's speed the process up this time.

I will take a very common I, VI, IV, V chord progression in the key of B Major and dress it up with common tones and arpeggiation. The basic chords will be B major, G# minor, E major, and F# major.

Example 5d begins the embellished version with an arpeggiated B suspended 2nd barre chord. Moving the root note from B to G# for bar two makes it a minor eleventh chord. This is not a barre chord, so the index finger only needs to fret the B string.

Replacing the E major chord is the Bsus2 chord, but with an open E string bass note. This combination contains notes from an EMaj13 chord (without the 3rd and 7th).

For the final measure, lift your barred index finger vertically to include the low E string at the 2nd fret.

The finished progression is reminiscent of the Dokken song, *Slippin' Away*.

Example 5d:

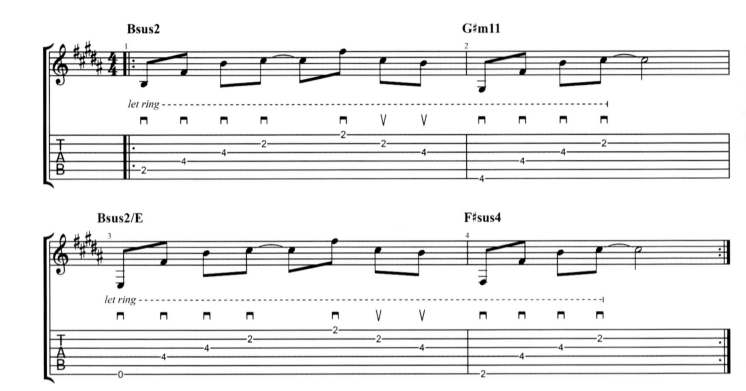

Instead of replacing the basic chords with embellishments, let's layer them together.

Here's a chord progression in the key of G Major. In a moment, I'll create an arpeggiated part that a second guitar can play.

Example 5e:

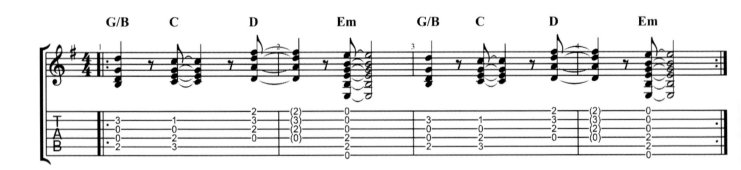

To contrast the approach of changing chord shapes, we can add another guitar part that uses static notes pedalled over each chord, played between moving bass notes.

Example 5f indicates slightly different chord names that reflect the common tones added to the arrangement.

On the audio for this example, you'll hear the chord part from Example 5e beneath.

Example 5f:

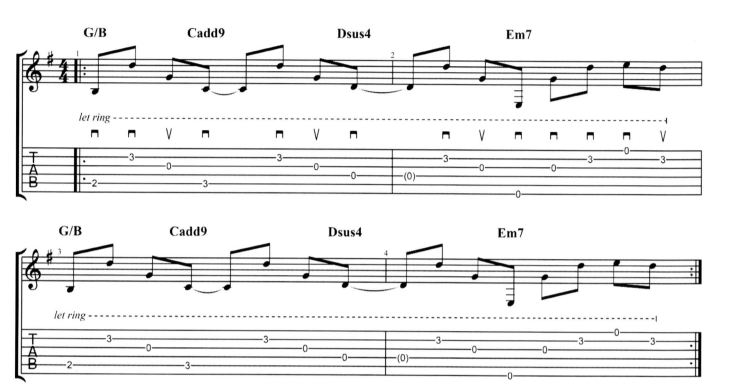

Here's a comparison between a single, repeated pedal phrase (Example 5g) versus alternating phrases (Example 5h).

With a chord progression of A minor, F major, C major and G major (from the key of C major), first up is a simple two-note pedal consisting of the notes C and G, on the B and G strings.

Let all the notes ring together as a chord, rather than sounding like a single-note melody.

Example 5g:

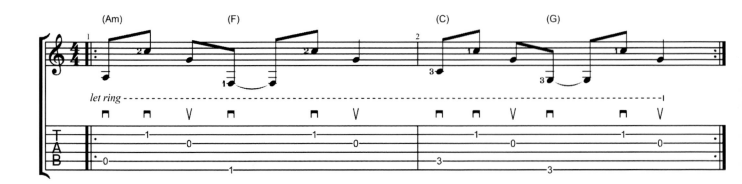

For this progression, I prefer to use one idea for the A minor and C major chords, and make a more developed melodic addition to the F major and G major chords.

Try this variation and see what you prefer. For a third option, play both versions, one after the other.

Example 5h:

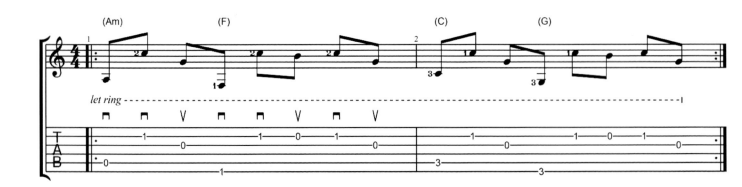

Static bass notes over moving chord parts were popular in many '80s arrangements.

Example 5i is built around a progression of C# minor, B major, and A major chords (key of C# Minor) with chord fragments on the D, G, and B strings.

While the chord voicings move down and up in two-bar cycles, a stationary sound is created with the C# bass notes (bars 1-4 and 7-8) and A bass notes (bars 5-6), both on the A string.

Reinforcing the stationary notes, guitar 2 on the audio track performs a slow gallop on the A string, doubled an octave lower by the bass.

Example 5i:

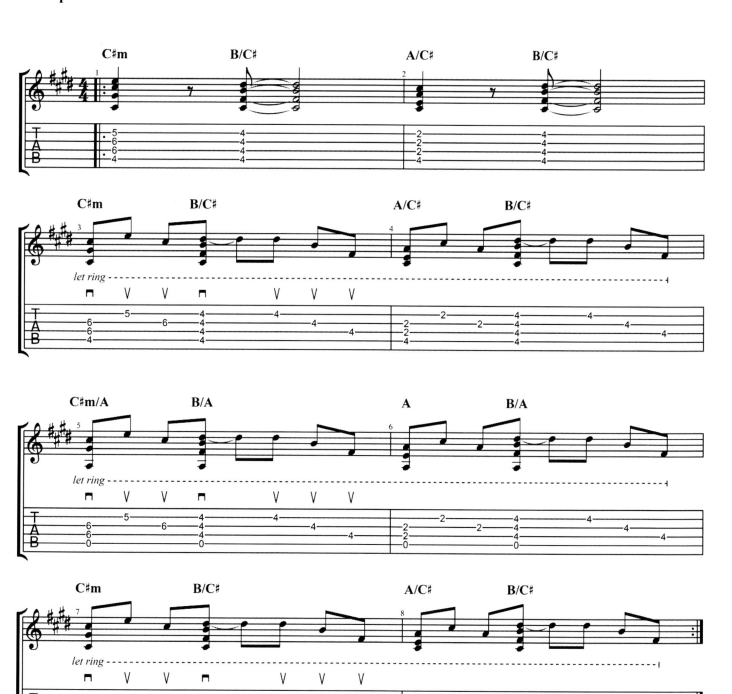

To imitate the second guitar part on the audio, follow this muted rhythm.

Example 5i2:

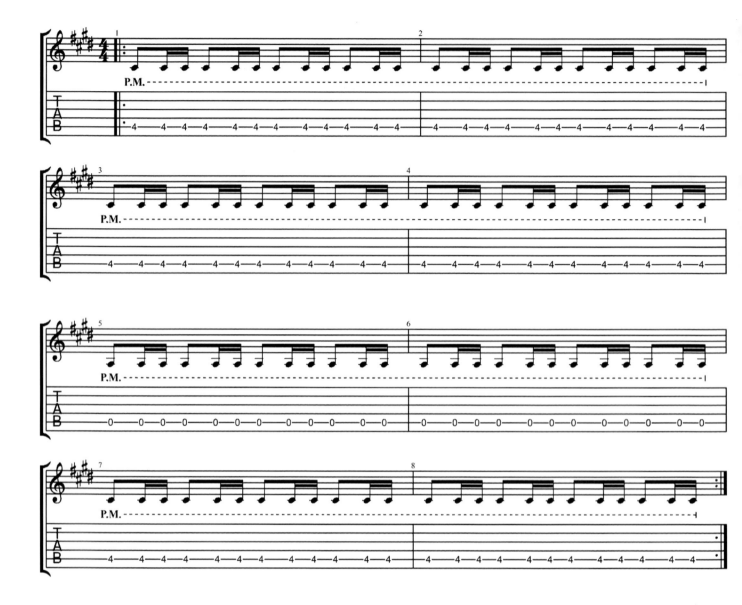

So far, we've looked at the soft rock and power ballad approach to clean guitar parts, but they also make great intros for heavier songs.

Played in the key of B Minor, here's an idea inspired by Metallica tracks like *One* and *Fade to Black.*

Example 5j:

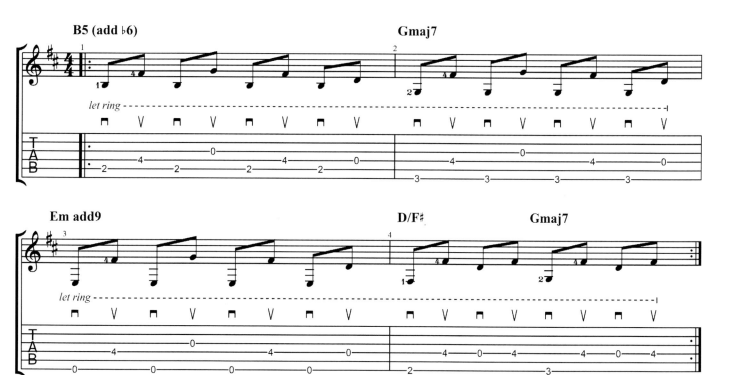

For the last rhythm part in the chapter, let's have some fun switching from clean to overdriven parts in the thrash styles of Metallica and Megadeth.

Written in 7/8 time, this rhythm part primarily uses the notes on the D string to indicate chord changes, rather than the upper or lower notes in each bar. "Slash chord" symbols indicate that the chords are moving, yet each is played over an A bass note.

The first chord, A minor, is outlined by the open A string, the E note on the second fret of the D string, and the A (2nd fret) and C (5th fret) notes on the G string. The B note on the 4th fret is a passing melody note.

The idea in bars 1-3 is to keep the notes on the A and D strings ringing while playing the melody line on the G string. Look out for a slight variation of the melody in bar three.

The chords change as the 2nd fret E note on the D string rises to an F note in bar two, then F# in bar three. Finally, in bar four, F major and G major fragments set up a return to the A minor chord.

For impact, as might occur in an actual song, bars 5-8 contain the same notes as the first four bars, but are played with overdrive, palm muting, and constant downstrokes.

Have fun playing with the contrast over the supplied backing track.

Example 5k:

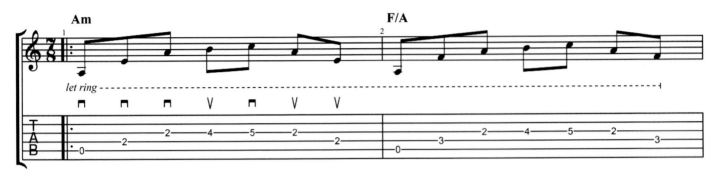

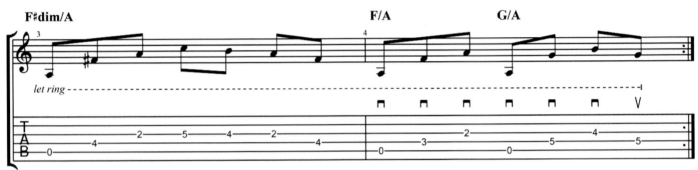

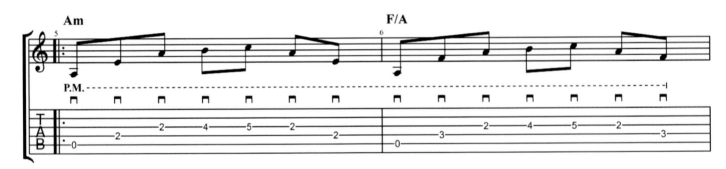

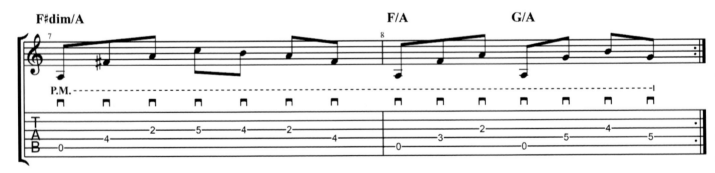

Tips for writing creative, clean rhythm parts:

- Know your key! What chords belong to it?

- Build a progression of basic chords that your part will outline

- Look for common tones between chords, especially open strings or notes that can be sustained or repeated across chord changes

- Arpeggiate your chords to give each note its rhythmic placement

- Repeat motifs on the treble strings while changing bass notes to outline a progression

- Try moving chord fragments with a static bass note

- Learn suspended chords and extensions like 7ths, 9ths, and 11ths to add colour

Suggested listening related to this chapter:

- Whitesnake – *Is This Love* (John Sykes)

- Def Leppard – *Love Bites* (Steve Clark, Phil Collen)

- Queensryche – *I Dream in Infrared* (Chris DeGarmo, Michael Wilton)

- Dokken – *Slippin' Away* (George Lynch)

- Metallica – *Fade To Black, One* (James Hetfield, Kirk Hammett)

- Skid Row – *18 and Life* (Scotti Hill, Dave "Snake" Sabo).

- Europe – *Open Your Heart, Never Say Die* (Kee Marcello)

Chapter Six: Scalar Riffs and Harmonies

Moving on from chords and dyads for riffing, this section focuses on single-note riffs using diatonic scales. As the examples progress, you'll need to call upon more dexterity and skills like alternate picking to add fire to your rhythm playing.

As shred guitar took its place in guitar circles in the '80s, flashy picking licks and sequences made their way into important parts of the songs, rather than being relegated to lead breaks only.

While bands like Iron Maiden and Helloween used twin-guitar melodic parts, emerging guitar heroes like Yngwie Malmsteen, Paul Gilbert, and Nuno Bettencourt unleashed riffs that were like picking etudes unto themselves.

Before heading into the next riffs, it's crucial to know major and minor scales across the fretboard.

Three-note-per-string scales are one widespread way to map out a key in all positions, so here are the seven patterns in the system, illustrated in the key of G Major. They are also the patterns for E Natural Minor.

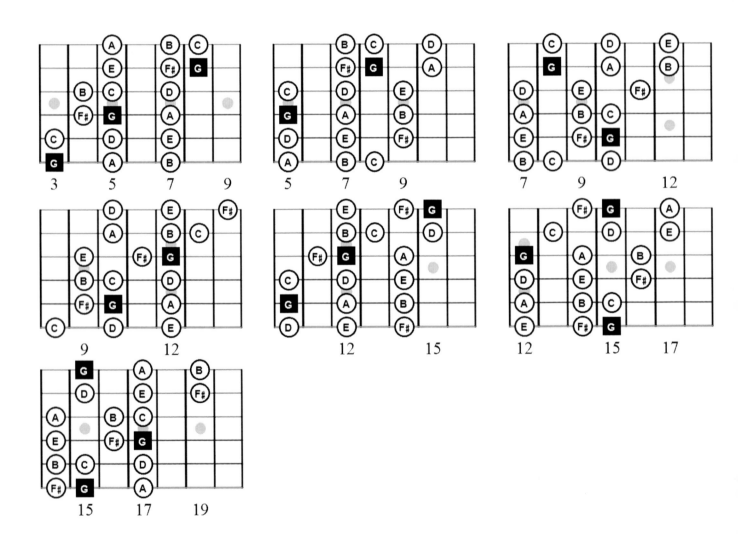

Besides learning scales in vertical blocks (box positions) as above, they can also be connected horizontally, using the range of the neck, on single strings.

Here's an Iron Maiden-style riff in the key of E Minor that move down positionally along the low E string. The longer 1/4 notes help outline the root notes of a descending chord progression.

Example 6a:

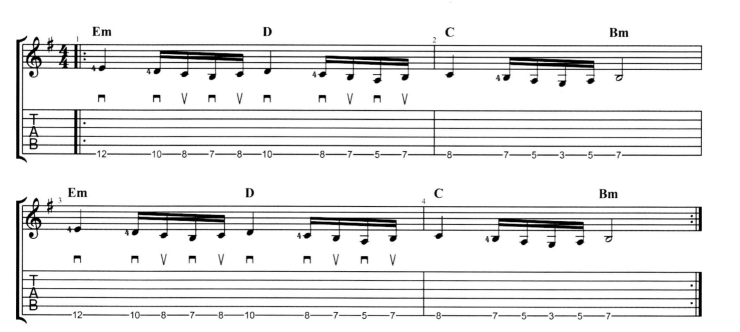

Many NWOBHM and European bands used diatonic 3rds to create a second guitar part as a harmony to the first. Diatonic means we stay within the key, and this means that some intervals will be minor and some major jumps, according to the scale.

Here's what a higher diatonic harmony to Example 6a looks like. On the audio, you'll hear the original riff in the left speaker and the new line in the right speaker.

Between the original line and the harmony, two chord tones are now spelling out the chord progression on each 1/4 note. The higher line travels down the A string, beginning on a G note – two notes higher than the E note that Example 6a begins on.

Example 6a2:

On the fretboard, it's easy to locate diatonic intervals for harmony parts. In the scale diagrams at the beginning of this chapter, play the second melody two patterns higher or lower than the original idea, then layer them. You can also start higher or lower within the same pattern.

Examples 6b and 6b2 form another twin guitar part, this time outlining the progression C major, D major and E minor.

The first of the two parts begins on the root note of each chord, while the second part starts on the 3rd.

In the audio, I play Example 6b in unison, but in the second version, you'll hear both parts, one in each speaker, with room for you to play the higher part with me afterwards.

Example 6b:

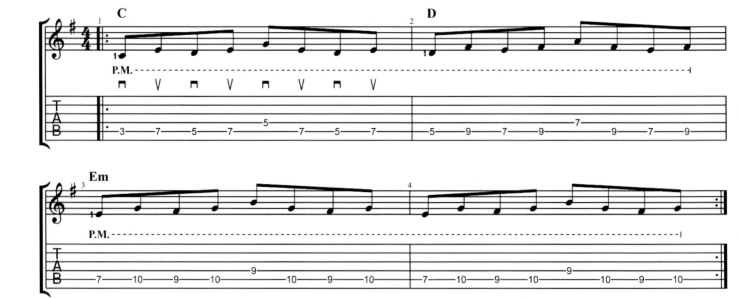

Example 6b2:

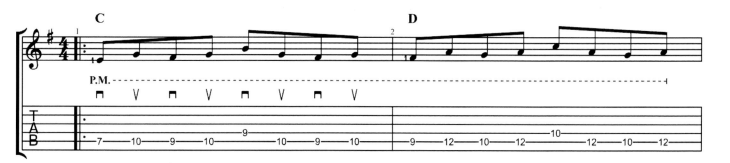

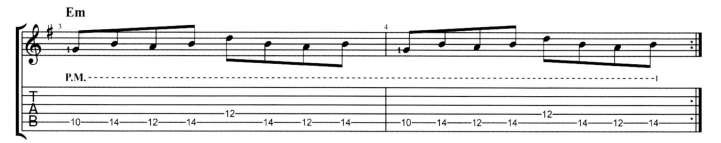

When the band Europe exploded onto the scene in 1987 with their smash hit *The Final Countdown*, most people associated the band with prominent parping keyboards.

However, two albums before their international breakout, Europe was very much influenced by NWOBHM bands, creating songs like the up-tempo fan-favourite, *Seven Doors Hotel*.

Here's a two-part riff in the style of *Seven Doors Hotel*. With the exception of the B7 chord (from E Harmonic Minor), each chord begins an 1/8th note ahead of the bar.

Each section of the higher harmony is played two scale patterns above the lower part.

Example 6c:

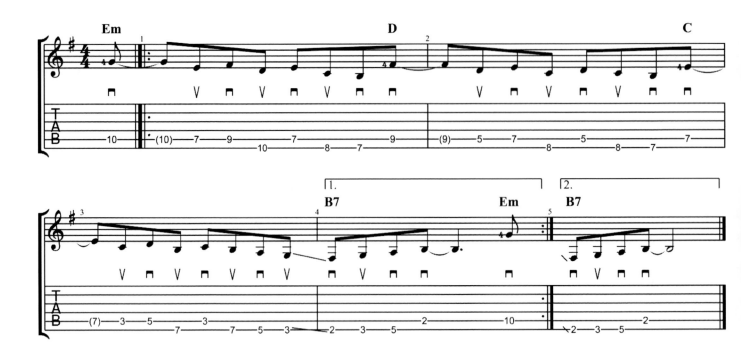

Example 6c2:

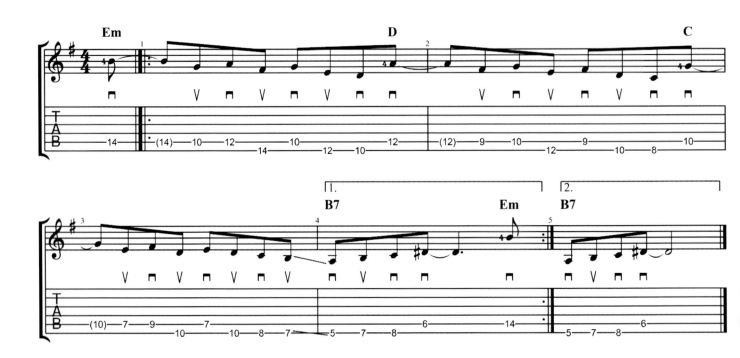

Hailing from the same music scene in Stockholm as the Europe guys, Yngwie Malmsteen made waves as a solo artist in 1984-5 after leaving the American bands Steeler and Alcatrazz.

The next riff is styled on Malmsteen's early solo releases, played in the key of E Minor with both the minor 7th and major 7th intervals used.

As with the previous three riffs, two guitar parts are played in diatonic 3rds.

Since the audio is performed at a slow metal pace of 75bpm, don't be intimidated by the 1/32nd note picking runs in bar four of both parts.

The picking of the final run is consistent with the Malmsteen picking system taught in my book, *Neoclassical Speed Strategies for Guitar*, but it can be alternate picked too, if that's your preference.

Example 6d:

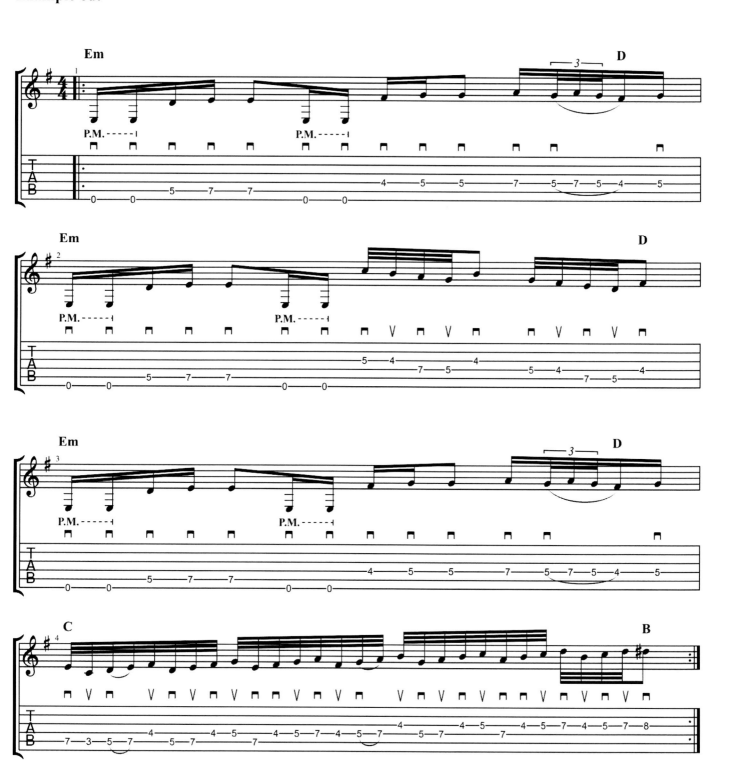

Example 6d2:

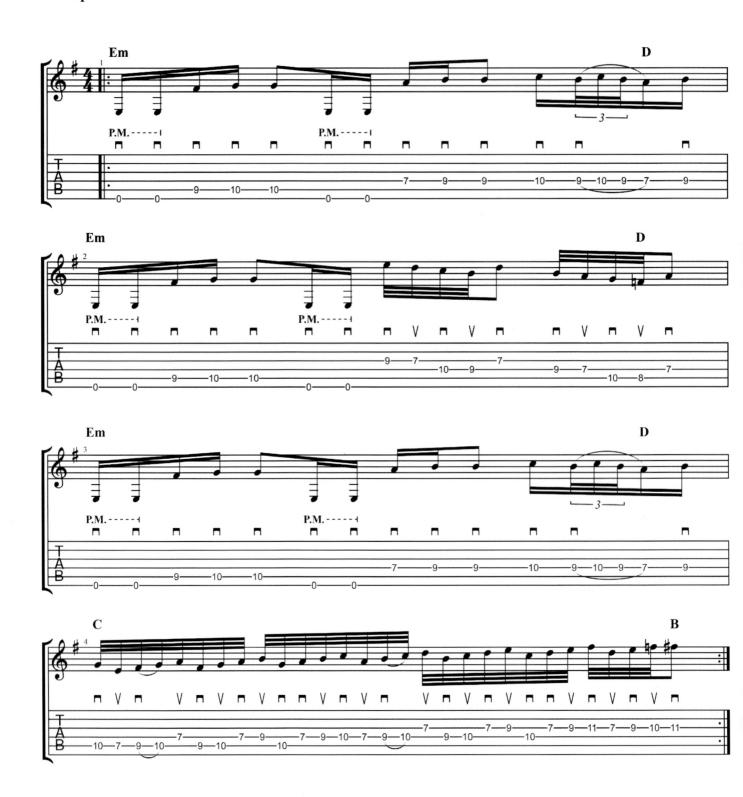

On the heels of Malmsteen came a barrage of skilled technicians playing what later became known as shred guitar.

74

Amongst the new scene that included Tony MacAlpine and Vinnie Moore came Paul Gilbert, fresh out of GIT. Gilbert combined flashy guitar with metallic vocal songs in Racer X, a band in the vein of Judas Priest but with even more focus on ripping guitar riffs and solos.

Incorporating his trademark lightning triplet picking into many of his riffs, Gilbert has a knack for high-speed bursts that add to the riff rather than diminish its rock edge.

Here's a Racer X-style riff in the key of E Minor. Look out for the switches between muted and unmuted notes because they play a big part in the dynamic range of the riff.

Example 6e:

All of the riffs in this chapter have used either the natural minor scale or harmonic minor variant. However, it's possible to write riffs modally around other tonalities and still sound rocking.

Example 6f takes place over minor triads but not as the VI chord in a major scale.

This George Lynch-style riff has an F# Phrygian tonality – the third mode in the key of D Major.

Featuring minor 2nd intervals (G natural) above the F# root note on the D string and low E string produces a slightly darker tonality than the natural minor scale.

In bar four, the riff is modified to work over the II chord in the key of D Major (E minor).

Example 6f:

The other minor mode commonly used in rock is Dorian, based over the II chord of major scale harmony.

Dorian starts like a natural minor scale until reaching the 6th degree, where it replaces a minor interval with a major interval. So, A Dorian (sharing a key signature with the G Major scale) contains the notes A, B, C, D, E, F#, and G.

The major 6th interval in the Dorian mode adds a more uplifting sound to this minor tonality than the Aeolian (natural minor) and Phrygian modes.

Paul Gilbert's post-Racer X band, Mr Big, put Dorian to great use with lots of interplay between the mode's major 6th and minor 7th degrees. Here's a Mr Big-style riff to demonstrate.

Example 6g:

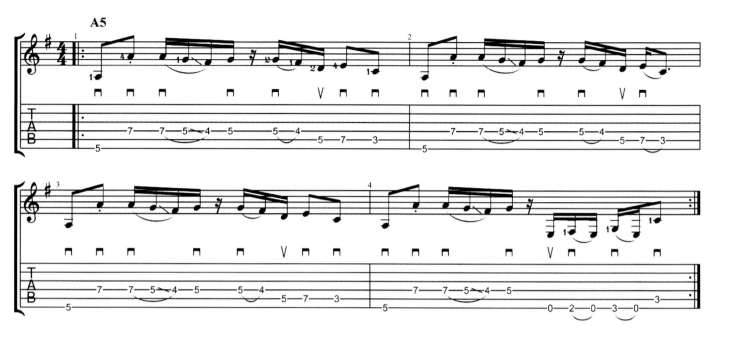

New York City band Living Color released one of 1988's most memorable riffs with *Cult of Personality*.

Here's a Vernon Reid-style riff featuring the G Dorian mode from the key of F Major. Watch out for the suggested fingerings as the riff jumps between the 2nd and 3rd positions.

This is played as a 1/16th note shuffle, so listen carefully to the audio to nail that feel.

Example 6h:

As the '80s drew to a close, more groove seeped into a lot of radio-bound riffs, as the influences of bands like Aerosmith fused with the chop-shop guitar style of the day.

Extreme's Nuno Bettencourt was one of the latecomers to the '80s party. Equipped with all the chops of the modern-day player with a penchant for songwriting, groove, and restraint, Bettencourt could take basics like the pentatonic scale and turn it into a lesson in dynamics.

With pull-offs, muted notes, and 1/16th note sextuplet bursts, Example 6i is a Bettencourt-style riff using the humble A Minor Blues scale.

Example 6i:

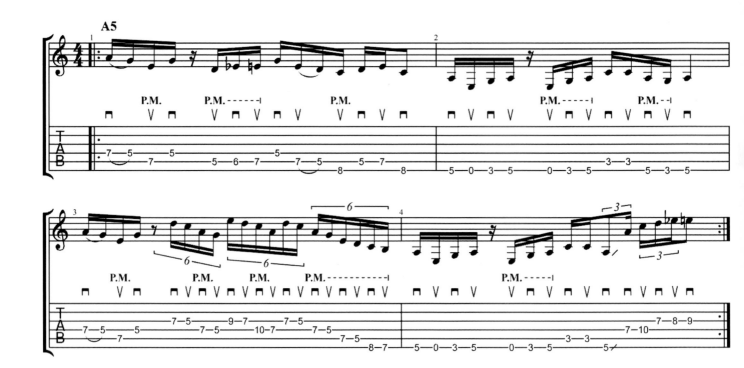

On the tail-end of the decade, 1989's self-titled Mr Big album featured Paul Gilbert trading and matching riffs with renowned bassist Billy Sheehan (Talas, David Lee Roth).

The two riff-meisters often played technical yet groovy riffs note-for-note with each other, inspiring the last riff in this chapter.

Using E Mixolydian (the fifth mode in the key of A Major), this riff is played with a 1/16th note shuffle.

The riff uses the A Major scale with a pronounced focus on resolving to E, using just enough of the triad tones of E major (E, G#, B), D major (D, F#, A) and A major (A, C#, E) chords to imply some harmonic movement.

We've already played some Mixolydian-based chord progressions in Chapter Two, but this riff approach highlights the use of a major-sounding scale with minor 7th degree.

Example 6j:

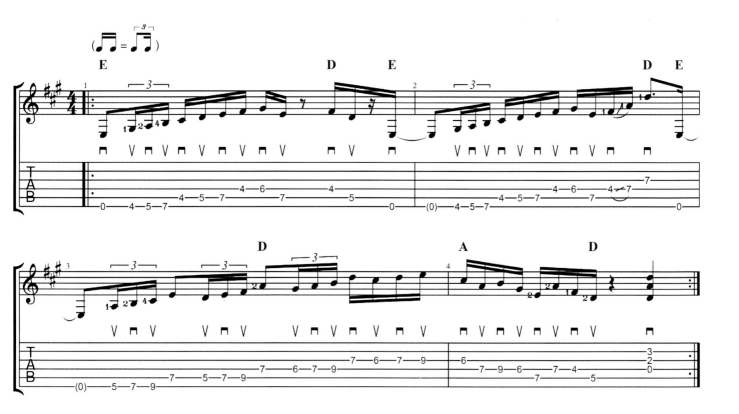

Now that you've worked through the practical content of scale riffs, let's run through my tips for creating your own.

Suggestions for creating your own scalar riffs

There are three things I seek out when creating my own riffs: rhythmic, melodic, and harmonic value. When I have all three and I like what I'm hearing, I know I'm heading in the right direction.

Let's start with the rhythmic element. I often do so because I feel that when it comes to phrasing, the *how* and *when* (rhythm) are almost more important that the *what* (melody). Even one note can sound great with the right rhythmic hook.

By replacing some notes with rests, even a straight 1/16th note rhythm can turn into something unique. For example, take a look at bars three and four below.

Example 6k:

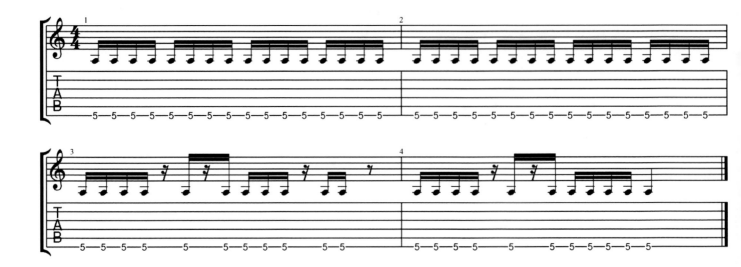

Building on the last two bars of the previous example, let's add some melodic content. To show you how effective the rhythm can be, I will just run up and down the A Minor Pentatonic scale.

You could approach the picking here in a few ways, but I opted for beginning each string on a downstroke.

Example 6l:

Since the original "riff" sounds pretty static in terms of harmony, let's make a few changes to bar two, focusing on some notes in beats 3 and 4 to outline the chords C major and D major, putting an Amin7 chord over the rest. This gives us an A Dorian sound from the key of G Major.

Example 6m:

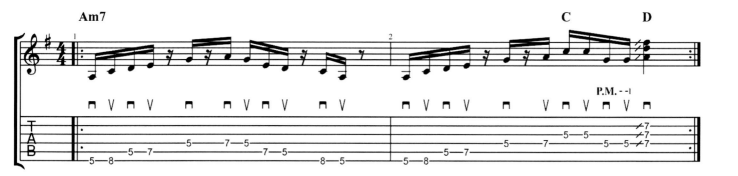

Finally, let's expand the riff by making it four bars, adding new motifs in the second half of bar three and all of bar four.

Example 6n:

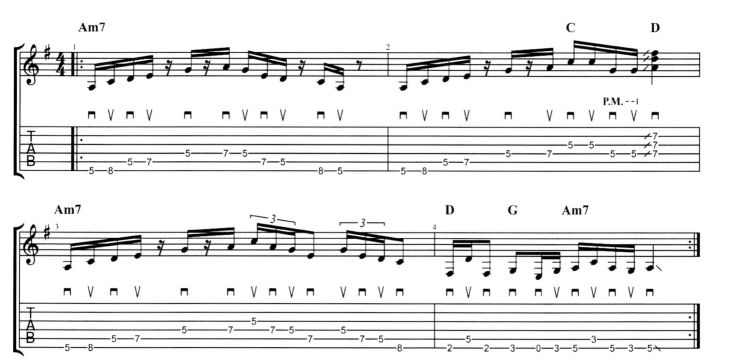

You might have already started with a small hook for other riffs and want to expand it.

Here's a basic pentatonic idea from the key of C# Minor.

Example 6o:

Let's say I want to fill those spaces in the previous example, but repeating beats 1 and 2 over beats 3 and 4 sounds a little boring.

What I can do instead is try displacing the phrase rhythmically.

In Example 6p, the idea starts the same as before, but then I repeat the idea a 1/16th note later in beat 3 and make the E note on the 2nd fret of the D string (beat 4) a 1/16th note shorter.

Now we've used the melodic content more interestingly.

Example 6p:

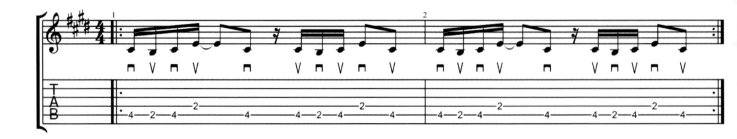

To extend the idea into a four-bar riff, add a new phrase to bar two, beat 4. Then, let's add some harmonic movement in bar four with power chords from the key and palm muting.

The riff has now evolved from a basic phrase to a usable song part in a few steps.

Example 6q:

On the heavier side of rock, you might prefer a steady pulse of 1/8th and 1/16th notes but want to add more interesting note choices to your riffs.

Scale sequences systematically move intervals or melodic figures through a scale to create motion and interest.

We looked at ascending and descending "fours" sequences in Chapter Four (examples 4k – 4m), so let's introduce some different approaches.

Here's a new base idea to embellish. It's centred on a D power chord, sometimes replacing the 5th degree with a minor 6th:

Example 6r:

Staying with the down-picked 1/8th note approach, we can replace the power chord chunking with a scale sequence.

Example 6s uses diatonic 3rd intervals in descending form. In bar one, beat 4, a G note follows the Bb note on the 8th fret of the D string, one 3rd lower in the D Minor scale. From there, each beat consists of the following scale note down from Bb, then its 3rd below, back up and so on.

In short, this sequence segment gives us the notes Bb and G, A and F, G and E, F and D, E and C.

Example 6s:

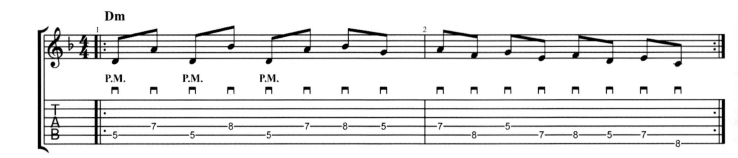

We can extend the riff by adding another sequence in bars three and four.

This time, I'm using a "seconds" sequence – playing descending diatonic 2nds moving up the scale: Bb and A, C and Bb, D and C, E and D, ending with F and E.

Example 6t:

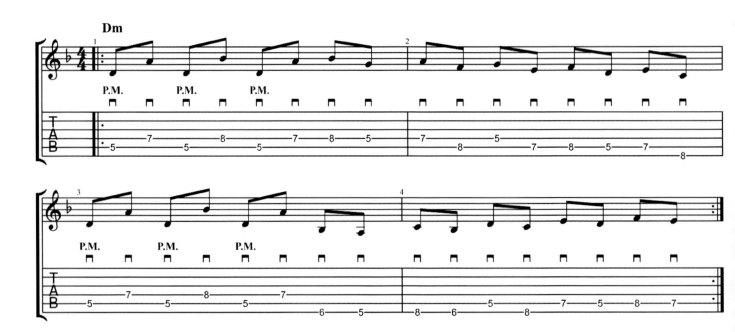

To end the previous riff, try this outro variation that introduces a faster sequence of descending sixes.

You'll hear me play Example 6t twice on the audio, followed by this ending.

Example 6u:

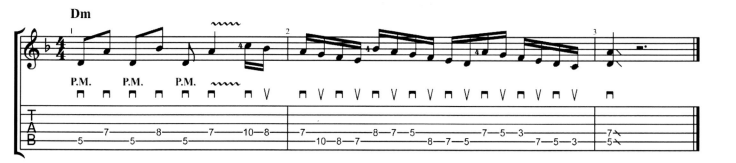

For the last riff of the book, I've written a short piece in the key of D Minor containing pedalled root notes, chord fragments, and scale sequences. It's played in the styles of Jake E. Lee (Ozzy Osbourne), Warren DeMartini (Ratt), and maybe a little Yngwie Malmsteen.

You can pick the scale sequences in your chosen picking system, but I've opted for economy picking in the indicated pick strokes.

The chord names shown indicate the overall chord sound created. So, while the notes C and E (bar two, beat 2) would indicate a C major triad in isolation, they're indicated as C/D (C major triad over a D bass) in the context of the entire bar.

Example 6v:

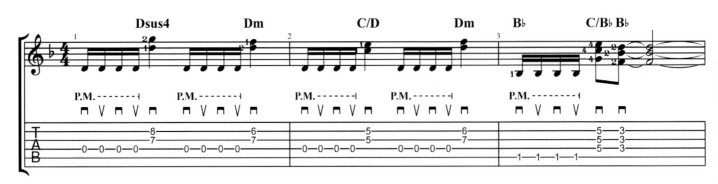

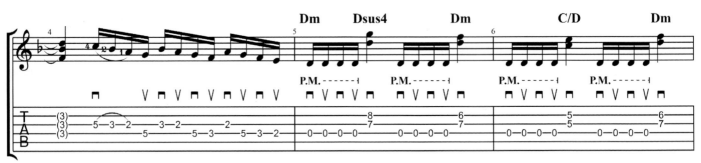

Suggested listening for scalar riffs:

- Iron Maiden – *The Trooper, Aces High* (Dave Murray, Adrian Smith)

- Yngwie Malmsteen – *Déjà vu, I am a Viking*

- Dokken – *Mr Scary* (George Lynch)

- Racer X – *Scarified* (Paul Gilbert, Bruce Bouillet)

- Mr Big – *Merciless* (Paul Gilbert)

- Aerosmith – *Love in an Elevator* (Joe Perry, Brad Whitford)

- Europe – *Seven Doors Hotel, In the Future to Come* (John Norum)

- Living Color – *Cult of Personality, Type* (Vernon Reid)

- Vinnie Moore – *In Control*

- Ozzy Osbourne – *Lightning Strikes* (Jake E. Lee)

- Def Leppard – *Pour Some Sugar On Me* (Phil Collen, Steve Clark)

- Michael Jackson – *Beat It* (Steve Lukather, plus the iconic Eddie Van Halen on the solo)

Conclusion

I hope you've enjoyed working through these concepts, playing through the riffs I've written and – ideally – begun writing your own using the ideas contained in these pages.

If you're new to these kinds of approaches, take your time. Your favourite guitarists of the '80s grew up in a different era, learning their favourite guitar parts from the 60s and 70s before coming into the fore with their playing.

The concepts I've used to break rhythm guitar into for educational purposes can be studied and practiced in sections, which will eventually inform several aspects of your rhythm approach. Applying them to your riffs will be where it all comes together.

For each subject, whether it be the pentatonic-based riffs of Chapter One or the shreddy diatonic riffs of Chapter Six, set yourself the task of creating some basic riffs using ideas in the chapter. Your first original riffs mightn't immediately be release quality, but composition and creativity are muscles that need to be built and exercised.

If you need some accompaniment for inspiration, YouTube has a plethora of drumbeats to jam along to and be inspired by. Search by style or even the tempo you have in mind. Listen carefully to the beats, imagine what kind of riffs would sound great over them, then start workshopping ideas until you find something that sticks.

If you have recording software, lay down your riffs and add other instrument parts. Pretty soon, you'll see your songs come together.

For added repertoire, the "suggested listening" tracks in each chapter are songs that you can seek out and study for further development.

Enjoy the process and results, and thanks for coming on an excellent adventure through '80s rock rhythm guitar!

Chris Brooks

About the Author

Chris Brooks has set new standards for the calibre of guitar technique books. With a flair for what makes things tick, his depth of understanding of guitar mechanics has helped tens of thousands of readers across the world.

Playing guitar since September 1987, Chris took early inspiration from Brett Garsed, Kee Marcello, Vinnie Moore, and Yngwie Malmsteen, practicing feverishly through his teens.

Educated at the Australian Institute of Music under the tutelage of Dieter Kleeman, Ike Isaacs, and Carl Orr, Chris developed a passion for guitar education that resulted in managing a music school with close to a thousand private students per week in Sydney's western suburbs.

Focusing on online education and product development in the last decade, Chris has now written a dozen bestselling guitar books, created scores of video products, and released two acclaimed instrumental rock albums.

You can learn more at **www.chrisbrooks.com**

Other titles by Chris Brooks

- Neoclassical Speed Strategies for Guitar

- Sweep Picking Speed Strategies for Guitar

- Advanced Arpeggio Soloing for Guitar

- 7-string Sweep Picking Speed Strategies for Guitar

- Legato Guitar Technique Mastery

- 100 Arpeggio Licks for Shred Guitar

- The Complete Guitar Technique Speed Strategies Collection

- Alternate Picking Guitar Technique

- Economy Picking Guitar Technique

- Rock Guitar Tapping Technique

- Chris Brooks' 3-in-1 Picking & Tapping Guitar Technique Collection

- 137 Guitar Speed & Coordination Exercises

- Pentatonic Speed Strategies for Guitar

Made in United States
North Haven, CT
22 October 2023